I Turned IT On...

Now What?

Discover Your Computer...
Recover Your Sanity

J. Wiltz Cutrer, Jr.

I Turned IT On…Now What?

Please direct requests for permission to make copies of any part of this work or to request the author speak at your event to:

J. Wiltz Cutrer, Jr.
206 Kitty Hawk Circle
Brandon, MS 39047

KnowIt@TechKnolutions.com

Visit us on the web:
www.TechKnolutions.com

Cover Clipart by Ron Leishman - https://clipartof.com/443438
Back Cover Clipart by Ron Leishman - https://clipartof.com/443435
Inside Cover Clipart by Ron Leishman - http://clipartof.com/448895

ISBN 978-0-9885928-2-7

Library of Congress Control Number: 2017907806

First Edition | 2017

Printed in the United States of America

Published by TechKnolutions, LLC, Brandon, MS

This Book is Dedicated To My Incredible Wife Kristen Pizzetta Cutrer

Throughout the journey of life, there are speed bumps, potholes, wrong turns, and missed exits.

I cannot imagine a better co-pilot than you, my love!

We may not always know what direction to take, but with you beside me, I know it will always be okay... just keep heading "north!"

∞ ∞ ∞ ∞ ∞

"There are 10 kinds of people in the world: those who understand binary numerals, and those who don't."

~ Ian Stewart

∞ ∞ ∞ ∞ ∞

Acknowledgements

There are countless people I must acknowledge and thank. Without their love, friendship, and support this book would forever linger in draft form on my computer.

Without my family, I am sure I would not be half the man I am today. To my wife Kristen, thank you for always giving me more than enough stories to write. As you always say, *"That's all fine, but if I break it, you have to fix it."*

To our son and daughter, Wiltz III and Izabella. Your skills and talents in this digital age give this old man quite a run for my money. Thank you for keeping me in line and encouraging me daily!

The hardest part of starting this literary masterpiece is defining a title. Taking to Facebook for inspiration from friends, I am thankful for Michelle Babin helping me refine the title, and Seth Whitehead for guidance on the sub-title.

As a lifelong computer nerd and veteran, I can easily write in acronyms and memes. I am forever thankful to those who helped me edit this from a gigantic run-on stream of thought into what you are reading today. Monique Uelmen, you are my RCA saint!

As I said before, countless people throughout this writing process meant so much to me in developing this book. The words Thank You do not nearly express all you have meant to me through this process! A special thanks as well to those who ask me the questions. Being a nerd means the first question I hear when meeting folks is "Can you fix my *(insert random tech item here)*?" This provides GREAT book material! LOL

5

Table of Contents

∞ ∞ ∞ ∞ ∞

"Man is the best computer we can put
aboard a spacecraft,
and the only one that can be mass produced
with unskilled labor."
~Werner Von Braun

∞ ∞ ∞ ∞ ∞

Prologue

Why does it seem technology goes out of its way to be confusing to so many? In a time in our lives when the focus seems to be on making things *"user friendly"*, we still seem to miss the mark when it comes to our digital connections. In our assorted professions we do ourselves no favors by making things confusing with fancy words. This frustration led me to create another book in the ever-growing *"Know IT"* family.

The goal of this book is to bring understanding to your technology challenges. While writing I was reminded of a mechanic-friend of mine. Recently I was helping him make some repairs to my vehicle (*i.e. I was in charge of holding the flashlight*) and as he was removing parts he took the time to show me what was wrong. When putting it back together he also took the time to explain what he was doing and why. I want this book to give you similar understanding. You do not need a mechanic to operate your car…you shouldn't need an engineer to use your computer!

Much like my other book, *"Don't Throw IT, Get to Know IT"*, I strive to deliver information to enable you to exercise power over your devices. By breaking through the techno-code, we will teach you to make IT work for you. Finding and using a common language is vital to our success. This book will take us through several stages:

- Understanding what you are looking for in a computer

- How *"The Cloud"* can make your life less stressful

- Working with email to have a more beneficial experience

- Backing up your valuable data properly

- Protecting your family from identity theft

I based this book primarily on examples from the Microsoft® Windows® operating system. I know there are some of you reading this which use or Apple® or Linux. While the specifics may not be the same, the principles surely will still apply. At the end of the day, it is all about operating our systems efficiently. It is just like driving a car! While the buttons and knobs may be in different places, and the gas cap may be on different sides, they still really drive the same!

DISCLAIMER:
While I have made every effort to insert and apply FACTS,
it would not truly be possible without the insertion of opinion
as well. Some readers may still disagree with solutions discussed.
Guess what? That is AWESOME! We are all entitled to such.
My opinions and solutions are the result of MY experiences,
just as yours are…well…yours!
Furthermore, I have received NO compensation from companies for
endorsement of their products or technologies.
I am simply sharing my experiences in the hope I can help.

What is Inside the Box?

∞ ∞ ∞ ∞ ∞

*"Computers in the future may weigh
no more than 1.5 tons"*
~Popular Mechanics, 1949

∞ ∞ ∞ ∞ ∞

Walk into your local store and you will be flooded with the sights of so many computing options. Desktops, laptops, tablets, and all in one's (*all in ones have all components built into the monitor.*) line the shelves wanting your attention. So many foreign terms and assorted sales fluff bombard your eyes. You just want a computer, but there are so many choices, and prices, between you and the cash register. In this chapter, we will break down these choices in digestible chunks so you can make an informed decision.

Laptop *vs.* Desktop

One of the first choices facing computer shoppers is what format to choose. The ability of the assorted formats is essentially the same, but there are some differences. These differences are not in functionality as much as in the intended use. You choose your device based on how you intend to utilize the tool. After all, let us not forget that a computer IS in fact a tool. You would not want to purchase a screwdriver when what you really need is a hammer!

What questions should we ask ourselves when deciding between a desktop computer and its portable cousin? There are quite a few and we need to try to be honest when we answer them. There have been too many instances where I see people swayed by a shiny display or a smooth salesperson. We need to keep the focus on making sure we get what we need, else you end up disappointed in the purchase.

The first, and perhaps most obvious, question to ask ourselves is do you want the computer to go with you or will you want it to stay put in your office? While this question may seem simple, it actually IS quite complicated:

- Even if you currently leave your computer in your office, bedroom, or other corner of the house, would there be an advantage to you, personally or professionally, to add the mobility a portable computer could offer?

- Though you currently use a portable computer, do you ever actually remove it from the base, or does it function more as a desktop unit?

- Do you need to add specialty functionality to the device in addition to what comes with it from the factory (*typically required of those who do advanced audio or video work*)?

- What is your budget? While it would be wonderful not having the constraints of a budget, the reality today is that available funds definitely drive our decisions.

Before we get into addressing these questions individually, lets briefly point out the basic pros and cons in the laptop versus desktop debate. This is the *"30,000 foot view"* version, and then we can zoom in a little closer:

Laptop Pros and Cons:

- + Mobile

- + Wireless connectivity built in

- + Battery-powered

- - Higher purchase cost

- - Smaller keyboard

- - Prone to theft

- - Costly to repair

Desktop Pros and Cons:

- + Less expensive

- + Full-size accessories (*i.e. keyboard, etc.*)

- + Cheaper to repair

- - Stuck in one place

- - Wireless may require additional parts

As we can see, there are plenty of advantages and disadvantages. This decision is not a one-size-fits-all proposal. Nevertheless, by addressing ourselves honestly about our wants and needs we can arrive at a solution that will give us years of satisfying use. Did I say years? Yes! I believe that by making a realistic and honest decision up front you can get more life out of your equipment. After all, if you need a hammer and you buy a hammer, there is no reason to purchase extra drill bits.

Do I need to be mobile? Seems like a simple enough question, but it still requires us to think it through. With mobility comes freedom, but with it responsibility and additional risk. A mobile computer can follow you wherever you go, but is also more prone to damage and theft while in transit. It also generally requires you to have access to a wireless network connection to be effective. (*For tips on choosing and setting up your wireless network please read my book, "Don't Throw IT ~ Get to Know IT"...just a blatant plug!)*

What is your budget for purchasing equipment? Let us be honest...budget can be a major determining factor in your computer choices. However, let me inform you about the cheap models you see gracing the pages of your Sunday newspaper...you do not always get what you pay for, but you always pay for what you get! While they may have similar parts inside, the cheaper models typically carry shorter warranties, older or even outdated components, and may not have the long life expectancy you can experience with a more current model. This DOES NOT mean you have to pay more to get a quality unit. It simply means you need to evaluate based on more than JUST the price.

Are you still on the fence? If you are wrestling with this question, I would like to offer an option that may bridge the two sides. This option will increase the price but will give the benefits of both worlds. Laptop computers can be *"docked"* to provide full-featured accessories such as monitors, keyboards, and mice. The dock provides connections for your accessories. You then simply connect your laptop to the dock when in the office and remove it when requirements call for mobility. The cost of a docking station starts at $100.00 and moves upward depending on the level of functionality and features you desire.

Laptop Docking Options

✝ ✝ ✝ ✝ ✝

What Are All Those Specs?

One of the more confusing parts of purchasing a computer today is determining what bells and whistles you need. Of all the items listed on the side of the box, I would like to point out the ones I believe have the greatest impact on your computer. These specifications also may have a great impact on how long it takes before you are itching to replace your equipment. Making an informed choice now can save you dollars and headaches in the end. While the SPECIFICS of the information may change, in the interest of keeping this book relative beyond next year's model I will speak of these terms in general to help you to understand the concepts rather than the details themselves.

There are certain key components listed when we talk of specifications per computer model. These include, but are not limited to, the following items:

- Processor

- Memory

- Hard Drive

- Screen Size

- Video Capabilities

Processor. You will also hear this component referred to as the CPU, the Central Processing Unit. In essence, it is the brain of your computer. It controls the flow of your data, whether you are balancing your budget or surfing the Internet. It acts as a traffic cop, directing data to the various portions of your computer, such as memory, the screen, or the printer.

What do the numbers mean when we see the labeling for the CPU? Even as a nerd, I get confused on this subject! In the *"old days"*, it was much easier to determine the relative responsiveness of a CPU, but things have become much more complicated. Today we come up against things like numbers of cores, fancy nicknames, generations, and all around confusing information. As such, this is a difficult concept to explain in general terms. In addition, CPU manufacturers release new models so often that by the time I could print this book we will see a completely new model line! For this reason, I will simply explain a few common CPU components below to help you make an informed decision about which model is best for you:

- **Intel vs. AMD:** Intel and AMD are the two predominant manufactures of CPU's today. Is one better than the other? This argument is almost like two good ole boys arguing over Ford vs. Chevy. The bottom line is both companies make a wonderful product and you will not go wrong any way you choose. While I have my preferences, experience has shown both to be solid performers for home and business users.

- **Number of Cores:** This is a feature offered to consumers with little or no real explanation. Without getting into the technicalities, number of cores refers to the number of CPU devices physically contained in the overall CPU container. Think of it like a pizza...one single pizza can contain two, four, six, etc. slices depending on how you slice it. More cores indicate the CPU's ability to multitask. More cores will significantly help people who perform more labor-intensive functions (*such as video editing*) or video gaming. NOTE: When I say video gaming, I DO NOT mean solitaire!

- *Model Numbers:* I could write an entire chapter just covering the model names and numbers out there. It is like walking on a car lot and seeing all the available vehicles. Names such as i3, i5, i7, Celeron, Phenom, Athlon, are Ryzen are present and available by just walking into the electronics department. Quite honestly, the best advice here would be to do a little Internet search on the model(s) that interest you and see what people are saying about their performance. These simply change too rapidly for me to honestly and completely debate within these pages. When researching hardware specifics I personally find the site **www.TOMSHARDWARE.com** to be full of useful information to help me wade through the latest and greatest offerings available.

- *Speed:* In the past, companies put quite a bit of emphasis and advertisement dollars into highlighting the speed of CPU's (*measured in gigahertz*). With the introduction of technologies such as multiple cores, these numbers have become much less significant. I advise not to focus on these numbers, as they will not be as big of a deal now.

One very important thing to keep in mind when it comes to your CPU: It is NOT an easy item to upgrade or replace. This is very much a *"what you see is what you get"* sort of item. I advise people to purchase the best CPU that fits their budget if you want to maximize the lifespan on the computer. A simple analogy using the Intel iCore and AMD Ryzen series would be as follows:

- Intel i3/AMD Ryzen 3 = 4-Cylinder Car Engine
    - o *Emphasis on economy (price) while still getting your most common chores (email, web, etc.) accomplished*

- Intel i5/AMD Ryzen 5 = 6-Cylinder Car Engine
    - o *Versatile and capable; takes care of common tasks but can provide a bit more acceleration when merging onto the Information Superhighway*

- Intel i7/AMD Ryzen 7 = 8-Cylinder Car Engine
    - o *The muscle car of the tech world; when you need to put the pedal down and take advantage of all the torque and horsepower to get you to the finish line*

Memory. Also referred to as RAM, or Random Access Memory, this is the working part of your computer. Think of it as the top of your desk. It is where all your current working items reside for you to manage and manipulate. If your taxes are open or you are in the middle of a close game of solitaire this is where you will find it. Like a physical desk, the more area you have to work, the easier your tasks are to complete. Imagine the difference between the space available on a TV tray versus a large executive desk and you can visualize the problem your computer experiences with too little RAM. If your system run out of space on this *"table"*, it must then utilize the much-slower hard drive to work with items. This would be like sitting at the kiddie table during a Thanksgiving feast.

Example of CPU (TOP)
Example of Laptop & Desktop RAM (BOTTOM)

RANDOM TECH TIP:

It seems there is no shortage of competing commercials regarding cellular services.
Do not confuse "reliability" and "coverage".
Most companies have reliability in services.
Coverage can fall short and creates most connectivity problems.
When you evaluate a new carrier, ensure they have the areas YOU need covered. Talk to people in those areas to see how their experience has been before giving anyone your money.

How much is enough? I hear this question quite often and the answer is varied. Let me answer that question with another question: What do you plan to do with your computer? If you use your computer as most normal users do, which is as a glorified typewriter, (*for those too young to remember, a typewriter printed letters onto paper...with a mistake requiring the use of a lovely liquid known as* "White-Out" *to cover up our mistakes*) there is not much need, or advantage, to overloading this portion of your computer. However, if you heavily edit video, pictures, or music files, your needs will increase significantly. (**NOTE:** *Heavy photo editing does NOT mean basic tasks such as removing red eye or cropping pictures.*)

Well...that is all fine and dandy, but how much does the average user REALLY need? At the time of this writing, as a GENERAL rule of thumb I advise folks to have around 8 GB (*Gigabyte*) of RAM. This amount balances performance, cost, and efficiency. Those who use their systems more intensively would understandably require more. It is not unheard of for a graphic designer or video editor to use 32GB or more of RAM.

One other thing to keep in mind regarding memory in your computer is in several cases it can be upgraded. This is true for desktops and many laptops. (*See important note below*) In fact, I have been able to breathe new life into computers simply by the addition of a little more RAM, which can have a relatively low price tag compared to the performance increase. Personally, I use the free tools at ***www.CRUCIAL.com*** to analyze a computer for its memory requirements/limitations, as well as to purchase. (*I have had excellent experience with their product in the past, and have received absolutely nothing in return for making this recommendation.*) A free tool on their site (*Crucial System Scanner*) makes upgrading easy. It will tell you everything you need to know to make a wise decision when determining applicable upgradability. It runs from your Internet browser and is self-explanatory, simple to use, and easy to understand.

Screenshot from Crucial Website

✝ ✝ ✝ ✝ ✝

IMPORTANT NOTE:

*Many new computers, especially the ultra-thin tablet-like units,
have their memory permanently attached to the main board in the unit.
This permanently attached memory IS NOT
user replaceable or upgradable.
The scanner will tell you if this is the case with your device,
typically by saying it is an unsupported system for a memory upgrade.*

✝ ✝ ✝ ✝ ✝

Hard Drive. Choices in hard drives are much easier to describe. They essentially have to do with speed and space. These two items pretty much sum up your choices. Speed dictates how fast you can access data. Space indicates how much information it can hold.

A hard drive is essentially a file cabinet. It holds all of the items you work with, along with storing information long term for you to recall later. I find the analogy of a file cabinet is rather appropriate. We have likely all seen a file cabinet disorganized with papers sticking out all over the place. Likewise, we have seen those neatly organized. The disorganized option is what I find most often when I look at peoples hard drives while working on their computer.

The first specification of a hard drive that jumps out is the size. The larger the capacity the more information you can store. As a general rule of thumb, you can expect the following capacities from a drive 500GB (*gigabyte*) in size (*estimates ONLY*):

- 125,000 Songs
- 38 Hours of Video
- 80 Movies
- 100,000 Photographs

Along with size, we see speed indicated in RPM, or Rotations per Minute, on many older or less-expensive hard drives. This refers to how fast the hard drive is actually spinning inside its case. (*There is another style of hard drive, referred to as SSD or "Solid State Drive", which we will discuss later.*) The spinning computer hard drive is very similar to a record player (*younger readers, please consult someone near you with a few grey hairs for explanation of a record player*). It spins around while a needle-like arm floats above it at a distance less than the width of a strand of hair reading magnetically recorded information from the platter surface. The typical speeds are 5,400 RPM and 7,200 RPM. The higher speed drives offer faster access to your data at a slightly increased cost.

There is another kind of hard drive on the market known as an SSD, or Solid State Drive. This is the newest, latest, greatest, and preferred hard drive option in many of today's devices. It would be similar in size measurements but not measured in RPM, as it actually has NO moving parts. It is similar to the portable thumb drives you see people using. SSD's are typically smaller in overall capacity compared to spinning drives and are more expensive. However, they have a strong advantage in that they are MUCH faster, reducing things such as boot time (*the time it takes for your computer to be ready to use after you turn it on*) and the time required to open your files. They also to generate less heat, giving a huge advantage in the constantly shrinking portable devices we have today.

With the advantages of SSD, their shrinking price tag, and similarly shrinking devices...why do we still have spinning disks you ask? Simply put, spinning drives still have great advantage when it comes to storage size. While the SSD continues to catch up, the spinning drive also continues to leap forward, sometimes providing up to 8-times the storage space for a similar price. Depending on your needs, it still holds a place in your digital toolbox.

Interior Image of a Spinning Hard Drive

Interior Image of a SSD Drive

Screen size. This applies primarily to laptops, but we can also use this to relate to the value of screen size with our desktop computers. With a laptop, the size screen you start with will be the size you are using for the life of the unit. Make sure you choose one that works well for you. For those that are ordering a laptop online I would suggest a visit to a local store to view different size units and determine your optimum size.

Another current trend with computers and screens is the utilization of multiple monitors. With the desktop, this task is much easier as many can easily accommodate multiple monitors. However, the laptop user does not have to miss out when it comes to screen real estate. Most laptops offer an output jack to connect an additional monitor, or the more common usage of the projector when making business presentations. Additionally, if you use a docking station, most support multiple video connections (*typically maxing out at two, but you can get more depending on your budget*).

One small item to consider when you are viewing different models of laptops, and especially those with smaller screen sizes, is that the keyboards may or may not have a dedicated number pad. While this may not matter to you, it is a difference I felt worthy of pointing out for consideration. For users that need the number pad this can be a key factor in deciding between a larger or smaller unit. Of course, none of this will matter much if you use the docking station and connect a full-size keyboard as an option.

Keyboard WITHOUT Dedicated Number Pad (TOP)
Keyboard WITH Dedicated Number Pad (BOTTOM)

∞ ∞ ∞ ∞ ∞

*"As network administrator I can take down
the network with one keystroke.
It's just like being a doctor but without getting
gooky stuff on my paws."*
~Scott Adams, Dogbert

∞ ∞ ∞ ∞ ∞

What Are All Those Plugs?

Whatever computer you choose you will notice there are quite a few different spots available to plug in a virtual army of accessories. The good news is that generally, you cannot plug the wrong thing into the wrong spot. The bad news is that ACTUALLY you can...if you apply enough pressure and are willing to break things! Oh, and in nerdinology terms we call these spots *"ports"*.

Generally, the ports you see on a laptop are similar to those found on a desktop computer. While the laptop may have the same ports, you will likely notice the laptop contains less of them due to space restraints. The addition of the docking station as an option (*mentioned previously*) will usually add the additional ports you need to meet or exceed those of the desktop computer, allowing a laptop to become a full-featured desktop replacement.

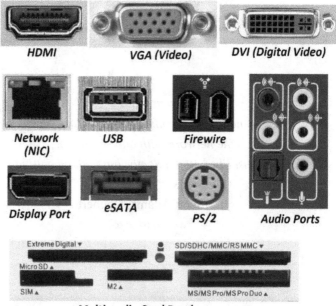

Multimedia Card Reader

Just Some of the Ports on Your Computer

What all those ports are for on your computer? They each have rather specific roles in bringing your technology to life. You may turn your computer around and find some or all of these ports. Depending on manufacturer there may be additional ones as well, these are the most commonly found:

VGA (Video Graphics Array) – This is a port commonly used to connect your display screen. The cables typically associated with this connection type typically have blue connectors on each end.

DVI (Digital Visual Interface) – Also used for connecting your display screen. This is a newer connector type typically found on high definition display units. Where a VGA connection uses an analog signal, the DVI connection is digital, resulting in improved clarity. While we mentioned that VGA cables typically have blue connectors, the cable ends for a DVI cable is typically white. These colors become a good method to differentiate what type of connection you are using.

HDMI (High Definition Multimedia Interface) – Yet another port for connecting display devices. Besides transmitting high quality video, an HDMI port can also provide audio connections. Sometimes used to connect to a higher-end computer monitor, the HDMI cable is more common when connecting to larger televisions and projectors. There is a variant called *"mini-HDMI"*, which is simply a smaller version as the name suggests.

Display Port – As if we did not already have enough display connections, here is yet another display port. This port differs in that it does not typically permit the direct connection of a computer monitor. There is often an additional connector (*called a "dongle"*) that will plug into this port to provide connections such as VGA, DVI, or HDMI. The purpose of this multi-use port is to permit the user more flexibility in the type of connection they use. As devices continue to shrink we also see a *"mini"* Display Port included on devices such as laptops.

31

All four previous mentioned ports deal with connecting your computer to a monitor. The quality of each option generally improves as you move down the list, with the fourth option, the Display Port, being able to assume the adapters for any of the preceding three choices.

USB (Universal Serial Bus) – The workhorse of the computer ports. USB ports connect everything from keyboards and mice to printers, smart phones, and tablets. Developed in the mid 1990's, this little port has grown to be fast, versatile, and included in just about every accessory imaginable. USB has many variants as well, with there being a mini and micro version.

FireWire (IEEE1394) – Originally developed by Apple, this is a high-speed competitor to USB. Typically, we use this connection type when connecting video equipment to a computer, as video files are large and require speedy transfer to keep people from getting too bored waiting for them to complete. *Not as common today*

eSATA (External Serial Advanced Technology Attachment) – Now that acronym is quite a mouthful! The eSATA port is the first cousin of the SATA connection located inside most modern computers. SATA is the way most disk drives connect within the computer, providing very fast performance. You may find this technology used with high-speed external items such as hard drives. The eSATA port is merely an external extension of internal technology, allowing you to connect items without having to open your case. It is definitely welcome when it comes to your laptop, which is where you will typically find this port type utilized. *Not as common today*

Network (NIC – Network Interface Card) – This is the port used to provide a physical connection to the network/Internet. The plug going into it, technically called an RJ-45, looks like an overgrown telephone cord.

PS/2 (Personal System/2) – Typically colored green (*for mouse*) and purple (*for keyboard*), these ports or referred to as "*legacy*" ports. Their purpose is as their colors indicate…they connect keyboards and mice to computers. As most mice and keyboards connect via USB, it is common to see these no longer utilized, though they do remain a possible connection option.

Audio Ports – While laptops may only simply have a single input (*microphone*) and single output (*headphone*) connection, most desktop computers will have more, as shown in the illustration. If you are reading this in black & white, I will give you a rundown of the standard color scheme utilized:

- Green – Audio Out; to connect speakers or headphones.

- Blue – Audio In; to connect an external audio source, such as a soundboard.

- Pink – Microphone In; to connect a microphone.

- Gold – Game/MIDI Audio Out

- Black – Rear speakers in a surround sound setup

- Digital/Optical – Shown in the lower-left corner of the audio ports and used to connect a fiber optic audio cable to a stereo system, typical for high-end audio applications.

On a laptop, you will generally see these ports using the same colors. If the laptop simply has black or silver plugs, look closely at the area. You should see a small image of a pair of headphones or a microphone. Do not be afraid to break out the reading glasses, as I have had to myself on occasion!

Multimedia Card Reader – With so many items such as cameras utilizing a multitude of media cards, the multimedia card reader has become almost a necessity to get the information on your computer. This unit (*as shown*) has the ability to read virtually any type of multimedia card you may have. One style rose to the top in popularity. The SD card, along with its mini and micro offspring, is the type most commonly found in consumer devices today. The SD card itself is the size of a postage stamp, with the offspring being smaller still. If you are using a laptop, you will probably have a port accepting this style of device and not the others shown.

This is by no means a 100% complete list of all of the ports you may see, but I am confident that it covers just about everyone and should give you a better idea of what you are looking at when you see the back of your computer.

✝ ✝ ✝ ✝ ✝

RANDOM TECH TIP:

Do you find yourself running out of available USB ports?
Consider using a USB hub to extend the
available amount of ports

✝ ✝ ✝ ✝ ✝

Brand Reputation

I felt it was worth the time to discuss the assorted brand names you see in your favorite computer department. The manufacturers out there may not appreciate me saying this, but in essence, the internals are the same when comparing similarly priced models between manufacturers. Sure, some have a better reputation than others do, but in the end, they do the same thing. The companies selling desktop and laptop computers do not manufacture the components themselves, in general. They buy them in bulk, often from similar suppliers, and assemble the final product.

If we use the analogy of a car we can realize that while the wrappings may differ, the generally functionality is similar. For your computer you turn it on, do what you need to do, and turn it off to use again another day. Sounds just like what we want from our car!

Does that mean that no matter which brand you choose you will get the same computer? Not necessarily. Turning back to our car analogy, we can see there is a difference in models coming down the line. While the general function is the same, some models are more desirable than a competitive product. Some do a great job of getting us to and from work while some are much more comfortable for the long drive across country. You pay more for the luxury model. It is many times the same with choosing a computer. You can get a basic model that will get the job done for less, but you may sacrifice options.

Am I saying you have to pay more to get a good computer? Not at all, dear reader! What I am saying is to look under the hood. Before you purchase, do your research. You would not walk on to a car lot and buy simply because of a flashy salesperson or the color of the car. You would (*hopefully*) read up a little, ask friends, and make sure you make a worthy purchase. While your computer may not be as expensive as your car, it does carry precious cargo. Think of the data that may reside within its components. Precious pictures, taxes, homework, and grandma's secret chocolate chip cookie recipe.

✝ ✝ ✝ ✝ ✝

RANDOM TECH TIP:

An important thing to remember when it comes to backing up information is if you back up a virus, you will restore a virus. Make sure you keep virus protection up to date to ensure you do not revive an old problem after an emergency.

FREE software such as that from
www.AVAST.com *or* **www.AVIRA.com**
can help keep you safe without breaking your wallet.

✝ ✝ ✝ ✝ ✝

Apple® vs Windows Devices

This debate will go on and on in chat rooms across the world long after this book decomposes and grows into a majestic oak tree. I will not get into the weeds on this topic as we could go on for eons. I will sum up the *"which one is better"* debate with a couple of simple points. At the end of the day, it is about what tool fits your purpose, budget, and preference.

- Windows and Apple® laptops both require and benefit from anti-malware software. One is NOT more immune or safer than the other

- Essentially the same software can run on either platform, though you should check any specific software needs you have before purchasing

- Don't compare a $300 Windows laptop to a $1,500 Apple® laptop, just like you shouldn't compare a $1,500 Windows laptop to a $300 Windows laptop; each tool has its purpose

- No matter the choice, YOU have to be comfortable with it. Make sure it is something you, or a trusted friend (*or vendor*) can help with should trouble arise

- Much like an imported car, an Apple® laptop can cost you more, once it requires repair. It is not a slur, but simply a reality

Warranties

Warranties are an item many people know little about with technology. While I cannot get into specifics for EVERY option out there, I would like to brush over a few of the finer aspects. I see many people struggle with the question of whether or not to purchase an extended warranty. This is a valid thought to struggle over, and one that warrants attention. *Let me also state that I AM NOT an attorney, so if you have serious doubts or concerns requiring that level of expertise please contact someone much more knowledgeable than me!*

Do you remember discussing the similarities between cars and computers? We can use the same comparison to highlight warranty options. Different models and manufacturers provide varying levels of support for situations you may encounter.

- Warranty periods vary in length of coverage, generally from 90 days to five years.

- Coverage may be for parts only or include parts AND labor.

- Some require you to bring the computer to the shop, whereas some coverage provides on-site service.

- Coverage to cover accidental damage may be an option.

You should base the level of protection you need on your usage habits and your budget. Extended coverage generally requires additional fees to be paid. For example, my recent review of computers at a local mass merchant revealed that most units came with a one-year warranty and required you to deliver the unit to a factory authorized repair facility. To facilitate returns you contact the manufacturer to report the issue and arrange, typically by mail, to return the device for repair. Depending on the manufacturer, it could take a week or more.

Upgrading warranties come at a cost. These prices vary between manufacturers as well as the stores from which you purchase the device. Recalling our car analogy, you should be sure to research the options BEFORE you step in front of a salesperson. This is information you want to be aware of in order to avoid an impulse purchase. Starting to make computer shopping a bit more involved than simply walking into the store, would you say?

∞ ∞ ∞ ∞ ∞

"Imagine if every Thursday your shoes exploded
if you tied them the usual way.
This happens to us all the time with computers,
and nobody thinks of complaining."
~Jeff Raskin

∞ ∞ ∞ ∞ ∞

Laptop Special Care

Did your research lead you to wanting a laptop computer? You are not alone. I am seeing quite a bit of laptops become the primary computer for families. With laptops, however, comes additional responsibility and security concerns. I would like to point out a few things you can do to prolong the life of your laptop. Following these simple tips, you can enjoy many years with your computer safely in tow:

- Cooling is crucial. The smaller structure of a laptop makes airflow a precious commodity. Paying attention to the airflow/breathability around your laptop can aid significantly in extending its life.

- Invest in a cooling pad. This is typically a USB-powered pad that contains fans and sits underneath your laptop computer, helping to keep it cool.

- DO NOT use the laptop on a soft and fluffy surface, like on a bed top. The blankets have a tendency to restrict airflow.

- Spills on a laptop can be a nasty (*i.e. expensive*) experience. Key components reside directly below the keys so damage can be quick and debilitating, along with expensive to repair.

- Physical damage is always a concern. Your laptops built-in screen is especially sensitive to pressure and drops. I have unfortunately seen the after-effects of a stepped-on laptop!

- Speaking of physical damage...too many people never think twice before throwing a laptop in a bag with textbooks or other heavy items inside. Make sure you use a padded laptop case when transporting your device

Your Head
in the
Clouds

∞ ∞ ∞ ∞ ∞

"What did people do when they went to the bathroom before smart phones?"

~ Aaron Cobra Mervis

∞ ∞ ∞ ∞ ∞

People often ask me about cloud services, cloud storage, and just the cloud in general. This seems to be the buzzword of the current Internet generation. Truth is...the cloud is not something new. It has merely moved out of the corporate datacenter and found its way into our homes. In this chapter, we will push the clouds aside and reveal the advantages, and precautions, when we start taking our technology to infinity and beyond!

What Is The Cloud?

This seems like a simple question, but if you ask ten different people you would likely get at least five different answers. Within technology circles, we define the "*cloud*" as anything that involves delivering hosted services across the Internet. These services share three distinct, and important, characteristics:

- Sold on demand

- Offer flexible amounts of service

- Fully managed by the provider

Sold on demand. This simply means you pay for desired services, as you need them. Additionally, when your needs change you are provided the flexibility to alter your services and agreements.

Offer flexible amounts of service. Flexibility is crucial to successful cloud services. The removal of cumbersome, long-term contracts or the "*one-size-fits-all*" stereotype allows the consumer to custom create a solution fitting their situation and budget.

Fully managed by the provider. This is, in my opinion, the single greatest aspect of today's cloud services. By the provider providing full support, the consumer (*or business*) is able to concentrate on his or her own needs without worrying about the complicated technology behind the service.

I mentioned in the opening that cloud technology was not truly new. While it may appear new in the consumer market, the principles and concepts behind it have been used for years by businesses across the globe. If you have ever worked at a company with a computer department, you have been the beneficiary of cloud services. That server room hidden behind some big door surrounded by a bunch of nerds with pocket protectors? That is the cloud as well. From that room (*or rooms*), a team of nerdy elves deliver services to you as you need them. Everything from providing you email service to a place to store your files can be controlled and distributed to you on-demand.

✝ ✝ ✝ ✝ ✝
RANDOM TECH TIP:
Have you ever been trapped in a group text message?
Although it can feel hopeless, there is a cure.
Go into the message and set the message "Do Not Disturb" option.
The group messages will continue to flow
but you will no longer here and see
the notifications sights and sounds.
✝ ✝ ✝ ✝ ✝

Cloud Popularity

Why have cloud services become so popular? Beyond the characteristics previously mentioned, the cloud has gained a foothold in the market due to its numerous advantages. It provides these advantages for business and home users, which I believe is the key behind its success. By bridging the home and office gap, we are able to see, and recognize, the advantages much more clearly.

- Ease of use for the customer

- Potential to reduce costs

- Allows access from virtually anywhere

- Offers continuity of service

Ease of use for the customer. This truly is important. When something is difficult to use the fact is that people will not use it effectively. Cloud services MUST maintain their simplicity. No matter how useful something is, if it is cumbersome to operate it most mill toss it into the dustbin of history that time forgot.

Potential to reduce costs. The stark reality these days is that we are all looking for ways to save a little money. Whether we are talking personally or professionally, cost remains a huge concern. Many cloud service providers offer their programs free to consumers, with many extending these free basics to small businesses.

Allows access from virtually anywhere. The ability to access your information and services from virtually anywhere shows the true power of cloud services. The fact is that we are a mobile society. Smartphones, tablets, laptops, and other items make it where we can be connected from just about anywhere we go. No longer does distance determine access. Do you need to access the files and programs on your home computer while at a hotel halfway around the world? You can do it! Do you want to carry on a video call with your grandchildren AT Disney while you are on a cruise around Alaska? Done! This and so much more is possible with today's cloud services. Moreover, often times you can do these things FREE!

Offers continuity of service. This is a concept not often heard when discussing home computer matters. Continuity of service is a concept employed by corporate technology departments to prevent an outage or loss of services from negatively affecting the business. Imagine how much of an impact each power outage could have on a business. Continuity of service means not keeping all of your proverbial eggs in the same basket. Reputable cloud service providers maintain more than one base of operations virtually eliminating the impact of service issues.

∞ ∞ ∞ ∞ ∞
"Uuuuuuuur Ahhhhrrrrr Uhrrrr
Ahhhhhrrrr Aaaaarrrrgggghhh"
~ Chewbacca
∞ ∞ ∞ ∞ ∞

Cloud Services

We have discussed many of the reasons cloud services are attractive for the home and office worker. We have talked about WHAT cloud services can do for you, as well as many concepts on WHY they are so important in today's society. What we have not discussed yet is WHAT some of the services are that are available.

DISCLAIMER: I am neither employed by nor compensated by the service providers mentioned in this section. For that matter, I have not been compensated for mentioning any of the products throughout this book. These are simply my opinions from years of experience.

Virtually every aspect of your computing experience has a cloud-based partner. Some of their functions you may be aware of while some others you may not. I will discuss some services that could make your life easier. Some of the more common services available include:

- Email

- Data Storage, Including Backups

- Social Networking

- Games and Entertainment

- Office Applications

- Remote Control and Access

- Video and Audio Conferencing

Email. I believe email services are familiar to most of us, though you may not have previously thought to classify it as a cloud service. Most home and business Internet Service Providers (ISP's) offer email services. These typically consist of an address on the provider's network, such as ***YOUR.NAME@provider.net***. They provide delivery, some level of SPAM filtering, and the ability to connect your email account to your home computer or smartphone. You can also signup for extra email accounts through providers such as Google® or Yahoo®.

Data Storage, Including Backups. If email is the most commonly known service, data storage may just be its up and coming cousin. Cloud data storage is a huge portion of cloud services growth. Face it folks…our data continues to grow. We will discuss cloud storage in-depth later in this chapter.

What kinds of data can you store in the cloud? Pictures, videos, PDF's (*PDF is a document designed to be consistently viewable and printable from any device using a variety of programs*), and documents such as Grandmas famous super-secret chocolate chip cookie recipe comes to mind. If you can store it on your computer, it can likely be stored in the cloud. (***HINT:*** *Be sure to check out the Frequently Asked Questions section at the end of the book for some cool picture-saving ideas*!)

Social Networking. Bet you did not think of your Facebook account as a cloud service, did you? All of those status updates, photos, videos, shares, and comments we upload into cyberspace sit among the clouds for everyone to see and read. Later in this chapter, we will discuss some tips to help protect your information.

47

Games and Entertainment. Not everyone would classify himself or herself as a gamer. Today's game systems are way beyond the Atari 2600 of the past, so you may be more of a gamer than you realize. Game systems and the networks they run across have become the multimedia backbone of your entertainment center. For example, my Xbox® does more than help my son save the world from a zombie apocalypse…it allows my wife connection to Netflix® to catch up on her latest shows and movies. Internet surfing, radio station streaming, and even interactive voting on assorted topics can be accomplished from the gaming systems of today.

Office Applications. Beyond the simple word processors of the past, office applications in the cloud can go all the way from virtual notepads to full blown financial spreadsheets. Using the cloud, we can connect to documents like never before. No longer are you restricted to a notepad and pen, or even a Post-It® note. We see Microsoft® putting their Office® suite in the cloud, integrating it with their cloud storage solution, OneDrive®, creating a powerful solution for their customers. Many others are using this power to their advantage. Products such as Ever Note® give you the convenience of a notepad on your tablet with the power to synchronize your documents immediately to the cloud.

Remote Control and Access. Perhaps the most useful to the user on the go, the remote control options available in the cloud keep you connected to home and work when you are away. One of the primary uses for remote control services personally is assisting family and friends with their computer problems. From any remote location, I can connect to their computer or cell phone and help them out. I can also reach back into my home computer to grab info for clients while attending one of my children's band events.

48

Another way I use this wonderful cloud service is to work from my personal computer when away from home. For security reasons I do not access online banking information from computers away from my home. When on vacation I will remotely connect to my house computer to check bank accounts, etc. from a computer system and Internet connection I know I can trust. We will discuss this feature a little later.

Video and Audio Conferencing. The smartphone has played a critical role in helping people see audio and video conferencing as a feature beyond the corporate boardroom. This area of cloud services has seen enormous growth in the personal and professional playground. With products from Skype® and Apple® providing tools to allow us not only hear, but also see the people on the other end, it is easy to see the reason for their popularity. In our office, we even use online conferencing services to conduct interviews! Imagine the savings in travel! Whether you need these services for business, or simply to see a faraway loved one, if you have not tried these services, DO IT!

Has anyone else noticed the "*theme*" of these cloud services? They enable us to work and play when we want, where we want, and how we want. Even more importantly is the fact that they enable something we sometimes struggle with effectively implementing. Cloud services give us a powerful toolbox to enable COLLABORATION. With collaboration, we can share our information instantly in ways that previously required couriers, trips back to the office, huge expenses, and other inefficient steps.

∞ ∞ ∞ ∞ ∞

*"The attention span of a computer is only
as long as its power cord."*
~ Author Unknown

∞ ∞ ∞ ∞ ∞

Cloud Storage

Storage in the cloud may very well be the most common subject I hear friends, family, and co-workers asking about these days. These requests go well beyond simple personal use. I believe that cloud storage is a major bridge for the blending of office and home tasks. Some could argue that this is a bad thing, as people may not disconnect from the office by physically leaving the building. That is clearly a topic for another book. The reality is that this bond exists. Since you have read this far I can assume you want to learn more about how to cross over and take advantage of the bridge.

How many times have you found yourself at home when someone calls needing an answer, and the documents you need locked away in your office? Even worse, you find yourself with one copy of a document on your home computer, a different version on a USB drive in your pocket, and a third (*and different*) copy on the office computer? Confusion does not even begin to describe the feeling. Cloud storage, by its nature, addresses these and many other problems in a simple, straightforward methodology.

Cloud storage providers vary in specifics, but most share quite a few important similarities. These parallels offer us a foundation upon which we can evaluate them to choose a solution that suits our needs. These will be crucial when implementing a solution:

- A starter amount of storage

- A method to increase storage availability

- Collaboration options

- Mobile device support

- Limitations to file types/sizes

- Method(s) to synchronize data

A starter amount of storage. Each provider will normally give you a basic amount of storage space to get you started using their service. This amount typically ranges between 2GB and 7GB, with 5GB being the average. This amount of space is usually more than enough for most cloud users. In addition to the starter amount of storage, you can gain more space (*discussed below*) up to a virtual unlimited amount of space.

A method to increase storage availability. The starter amount provided may be more than enough to suit your needs. In fact, I advise people to start by using the free space before entering into a contract to buy more space. No need to spend money for services you may never need to. If you do find yourself needing more space than the free base amount, cloud providers offer additional options. The two common methods are:

- *Referral:* For each new user (*friends, family, coworker, etc.*) you recommend that signs up for the cloud provider's services you receive additional storage space.

- *Purchase:* This is a straightforward option. You pay a nominal monthly fee for additional storage space. The amount you purchase is only limited by the amount you are willing to pay to suit your needs.

Collaboration options. One of the great advantages of cloud storage is the ability to share information with other people. Cloud storage providers have become essential in personal and business collaboration. Sharing a file or folder is as simple as clicking the item and selecting a sharing option (*actual steps depend on your chosen provider*). You enter the email address of the person(s) you wish to share with and set the level of permission you want to give them, such as view-only or able to edit. They will be notified and be able to carry out the tasks you assign. This can be invaluable to people working on a common project, or for those simply want to share documents and pictures with other people privately.

Mobile device support. With so many of us now carrying smart phones and tablets, getting your information on your mobile device is not only an expectation…it is a requirement. Each of the cloud service providers mentioned in this chapter will have a mobile program to use. From a business standpoint, this helps you have access to valuable information wherever you are. Imagine you are meeting with a client and information you need is not available. From the personal side of things this can be an enormous advantage as well, allowing you to keep your information handy.

Limitations to file types/sizes. While cloud storage is incredibly versatile, it also has limitations. Most providers will not limit the types of files you can store in their cloud solution. However, they will sometimes place limits on the file sizes. The primary reason for this is to eliminate people's ability to store illegal files, such as movies, and then share them with others.

Method(s) to synchronize data. Synchronizing data refers to the act of taking your information from your computer and getting it to the cloud. While all cloud providers will allow you to visit their website and upload your files, the simplest and most convenient way is with a small synchronization program installed on your computer. This program creates a special folder on your computer. Any items placed in this folder automatically upload to the Internet for placement in your provider's cloud storage solution.

The data synchronization process has an added benefit. Since it synchronizes data by making a copy, it is essentially a *"poor man's"* backup, as there are two (*or more, depending on how many computers you synchronize with*) copies of each of your items. HOWEVER, let me state that while it is true that you will end up with multiple copies in separate locations, I do NOT believe this is an advisable *primary* backup solution. We will be discussing data backup in further detail in a later chapter.

52

Cloud Providers

Who are some of the major players when it comes to cloud storage? The good news is that you have plenty of choices. The bad news is that you have plenty of choices! I will list and briefly discuss SOME of the players in the game below along with some of their advantages and disadvantages. While there are more than I list here, I have chosen these based on my own experiences with their offerings:

- Google® Drive

- Microsoft® OneDrive

- Apple® iCloud

- Dropbox

- Amazon Cloud Drive

DISCLAIMER:
Limitations and features are subject to change!
These providers can change anytime,
so always check first!
Enhanced features are typically
available for a nominal fee

Google® Drive®. It may come as no surprise to many of you to see Google® on this list. Google® is a cornucopia of cloud services, with storage being just one of their offerings. The integration of Google® with so many other programs such as Gmail, along with the fact that so many already have a free Gmail account, makes Google® Drive® a popular service. It has a simple interface already familiar with many Google® fans. Some key features include:

- Provides 15 GB of initial free storage

- Additional storage space must be purchased

- Tracks all changes for prior 30 days to items, allowing you to restore a previous version of the item

- Attach documents in your Google® Drive® to Gmail emails to easily send large attachments with ease

Microsoft® OneDrive®. Not one to be outdone, Microsoft® also has a solution for cloud storage. In newer versions of Microsoft® Office, we see even more cloud storage integration in that you can directly save all of your Word and Excel documents directly to the Microsoft® cloud solution. Some key features include:

- Provides 5 GB of initial free storage

- Additional storage space can be purchased, as well as gained through bundling of other services such as Office 365

- Allows creation and editing of Microsoft® documents directly within OneDrive on the Internet, no app required

- Does NOT currently track file version changes

Apple® iCloud. Anyone with an Apple® product has automatic access to iCloud services. The Apple® cloud solution integrates with Apple® devices allowing you to back up your contacts, pictures, music and more to your iCloud account. While this provides easy backup to your iDevice, it can go even further to store your key information. Some key features include:

- Provides 5 GB of initial free storage

- Additional storage space can be purchased

- Provides backup of your iDevices

- Geared primarily for Apple® devices

- Integrates directly with applications on your iDevice

Dropbox®. The granddaddy of the cloud storage providers, Dropbox® was one of the first public providers reaching out to consumers. Simplicity is truly the name of the game when it comes to cloud storage and Dropbox® is no exception. The referral system to provide more storage was popularized by Dropbox®, with the possibility to earn up to 16 GB of free storage with enough referrals signing up for Dropbox® accounts. Some key features include:

- Provides 2 GB of initial free storage

- Additional storage can be bought or earned by referring friends to the service

- Encrypts your files for security

- Keeps track of any changes over previous 30 days, allowing you to restore a previous version of the item

You are probably wondering, "*What's The Catch?*" There is sometimes a "*price*" for utilizing free services such as those mentioned here. This typically comes in the form of advertisements. For example, it should come as no surprise that Google® is an advertising company. The revenue needed to provide their many services comes from your search information, browser history, and other info they gather for the purposes of showing targeted ads while you are using online services. Have you ever noticed that if you are searching for a vehicle you will suddenly notice the many ads on different pages for automotive sales? That is the advertising aspect of "*free*" hard at work. That is why it is important to READ before accepting online agreements. It is safe to say that even using the most basic of online services will at least minimally expose you to such marketing tactics.

RANDOM TECH TIP:
Every heard of an OBD-II Adapter? It is a direct link
to the computer in your vehicle.
You can plug it in those manufactured after 1996 to read diagnostic
information such as fuel economy, troubleshoot problems,
and even automatically dial emergency services
in case of an accident.
One popular and full-featured adapter is the "Automatic Pro" which
links to your Bluetooth-enable smart phone to provide
you extensive insight and features.

✝ ✝ ✝ ✝ ✝

Remote Control in the Cloud

With remote control across the cloud, we enable the office and house to extend well beyond our basic borders. I cannot count how many times this simple yet powerful cloud service has saved me a trip across town to rescue a friend in a technical emergency. With a few simple clicks, I can connect to their computer safely and securely, and see exactly what they see. I can even take full control and repair any issue they are experiencing.

Remote control across the Internet has many uses beyond rescuing my mother-in-law from the latest popup virus or fixing my wife's email issues. There are many times when remotely connecting to another device can be to your advantage. In addition, with current cloud offerings this is even possible from your smart phone or tablet device. Just a few of the advantages to using a cloud remote control service are:

- Access your computer while away

- Demonstrate procedures to others

- Perform work tasks

- Conduct and attend meetings

Access your computer while away. Have you ever been away and needed to get back to your computer for an important file? I have already mentioned how I often use this feature to provide my mother-in-law and wife with computer support. This key feature comes in handy many other times. For example, I remotely connect to my home computer when I am away on vacation to check on financial items such as my bank account. Why, you ask? As I discussed in my previous book, I do not trust Internet connections that I do not control. Areas such as hotels and coffee shops can have plenty of digital stalkers waiting to steal information. By connecting through a SECURE connection to my home, I can access information with far less fear of digital pirates hijacking my data.

Demonstrate procedures to others. Have you ever been working on something and had to explain it to someone across a telephone? It can be a difficult and frustrating task. With a remote control connection, you can share your screen with others so they can see what you see, enabling much easier communication. You can use this feature to show someone how to perform a task on a computer or to help kids with their online homework. You limit your possibilities only by your needs. We can all agree that any task is easier when you can see what you need to see.

Perform work tasks. Unfortunately, we cannot escape the fact that work seems to follow us home, just as home seems to creep into the office. It is frustrating being at home and needing to get some task accomplished for the office. The time it takes to get dressed, get there, and return home is many times more (*in most cases*) than the time taken to perform the task. It becomes much easier if you can hop on your computer, reach into the office electronically, and tend to the task. You can then get back to relaxing with the family. I cannot begin to count how many times this has saved me literally hours of drive and prep time to tend to last-minute or urgent necessities.

Conduct and attend meetings. This does not have to be only work related. This can be on a personal level as well. Have you ever attended a meeting online? It is not as cumbersome and complicated as many seem to think. It is rather simple. It allows you to show things such as PowerPoint® presentations and videos to multiple people simultaneously. It enables video and audio chat between attendees. It can even provide recordings of the session to refer to later. You can even attend these meetings from your mobile device. Of course, there is always just the nice personal touch of carrying on a conversation while being able to see the person(s) you are talking to no matter how far away they may be.

So now, we know the things we can do with a cloud-based remote control program, but who are some of the players in the game? While there are quite a few options out there, two have stood out with me as simple to use, reliable, and full of plenty of features to meet just about anyone's needs. These options are free for personal usage, while they provide services for businesses at a nominal charge.

For my remote control purposes, I use either TeamViewer (*www.TEAMVIEWER.com*) or LogMeIn (*www.LOGMEIN.com*). Both of these have proven themselves over the years as easy to use and reliable. In addition, with their simple to use app on your smartphone or tablet you are always in touch with your computer(s)…or a friend, or relative's computer if called upon to use your knowledge to help others with their technical challenges.

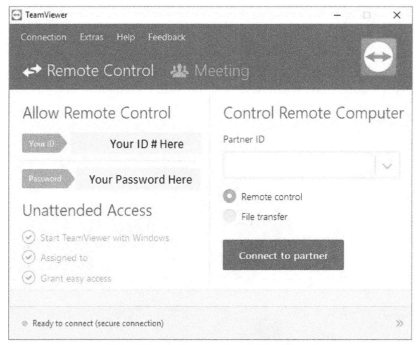

TeamViewer Remote Control Interface

Safety amongst the Clouds

A constant concern when utilizing cloud services is the safety and security of your information. It is a very important question, and one that imitates the proverbial moving target. Looking through the news today will give us plenty of examples of public backlash when companies change their privacy policies. Facebook sees itself constantly under fire. With almost 2 billion users, they are an attractive target for people wanting to harvest information. With the amount of information that people reveal on their pages it also highlights the need to be especially vigilant. We will discuss privacy concerns in a later chapter, but I wanted to point out a few items while we were here.

- Terms of service

- Data ownership

- Provider reputation

- Access control

Terms of service. Have you read the terms of service of the provider? Amazingly, most people pass right by this legal document and move on ahead, not knowing what it is you are agreeing to allow with your information. The terms of service are crucial to establishing a level of understanding and trust. They will cover issues such as acceptable uses of the service by you or your business. This defines how you can use the service, personally and professionally. They will also describe to what extent the service provider can use your information. For example, it will state whether they can sell your contact information for marketing purposes or use your pictures for advertisements, along with any copyright conveyance. A somewhat amusing, though true, example of people agreeing to things they never read is in the Apple® End User License Agreement (EULA):

https://www.apple.com/legal/internet-services/itunes/appstore/dev/stdeula/

"You also agree that you will not use these products for any purposes prohibited by United States law, including, without limitation, the development, design, manufacture or production of nuclear, missiles, or chemical or biological weapons."

The good news is this means that countries such as North Korea cannot use their iPad for the development of weapons of mass destruction. The question I ask myself, however, is what lead to the need of including such a statement?

Data ownership. Who owns the data once you upload it to a cloud service provider? Can they use your information? We see this question come up especially in regards to pictures uploaded to assorted cloud services. We are a visual society, and if you are like me, you like to keep those pictures of your life exactly that…yours! I consider even my kids school pictures to be confidential, only worthy of sharing with those I choose. Your standards may vary, so keep this in mind when reviewing their terms of service.

Provider reputation. Seems like a simple question, but it is a vital one to the safety and security of your information. Primarily, a provider without a good reputation is NOT someone you want to trust with your information. We cannot lose sight of the fact that data IS money. Even something as simple as your email address along with your name is enough to bring a couple of bucks to a crooked vendor. Luckily, there are plenty of reputable vendors playing in the cloud.

We can see an example of this in the story of Megaupload, a cloud service used by people worldwide to upload large files for sharing with others across the Internet. On the surface, this may seem like a helpful and reputable service idea. The problem came in that many used Megaupload to host illegal files, such as pirated music and movies, for redistribution. Eventually this illegal purpose caught up to them and they had all of their equipment seized. While this took quite a bit of illegal material down, individuals and businesses that chose to use their services for legal purposes found their materials seized as well.

The moral of this story is be careful who you trust with your information. While no one is perfect, you want a provider that does their best to protect you and your information. You would not trust just anyone with your credit cards, driver's license, car, or spouse. Treat your data with the same level of care.

Access control. One advantage of clouds services is the availability of your information from virtually anywhere. This can also become a disadvantage. If you add applications to your smart phone, tablet, or laptop to access your cloud-stored information you should be mindful of the fact that if you lose these portables items someone else can gain this same access. It is therefore important that we mention the importance of a password to protect your data.

How about password protection for your smart phones and tablet? These are actually rather simple to set up, though many people fail to do so because they consider the password to be an inconvenience. How much more troublesome would it be to have all of your information gone through by a stranger in case of loss or theft? With setting a password being as simple as it is, there really is no excuse for not having this protection in place on any device. For a more in-depth discussion on passwords, please refer to my other book, *"Don't Throw IT ~ Get To Know IT"*.

Generally, a password on a smart phone or tablet will consist of a series of numbers, similar to your bank PIN, or a visual pattern where you drag your fingers over dots in a pattern of your own design. We see the number pattern typically on Apple® iDevices while the visual pattern seems to be most common on Android-based devices. One setting that I would recommend is the one that will erase the devices data after a number of failed attempts. This will prevent someone from continuing to guess until guessing it right. As long as you regularly backup your device (*typically by plugging it into your computer, or synchronizing to the providers cloud services*) the risk to you for data loss is minimal. In addition, I would recommend NOT setting the code to the same as your bank PIN. It is just not good security practice, because if they compromises one, they would automatically have the other one.

What about thumbprints, which have become so common on our mobile devices? I think these are great tools in keeping your information safe. We must be careful not to consider this the final exclamation point on security. Did you know a gummy bear COULD compromise your thumbprint? It is true! Think about it: You leave a slight oily duplicate of your fingerprint behind when you press your thumb to open the phone. A gummy bear is about the same consistency as your thumb. Consequently, an enterprising crook could press that gummy against the scanner and unlock your phone, while having a quick snack, to steal your data. Do not doubt it…it has happened!

As simple as that sounds, it is even simpler to prevent. When pressing your thumb to unlock your device swipe away (*i.e. drag your finger against the button rather than lifting off*) therefore smearing your print and sending those yummy gooey bears back to the snack drawer where they belong.

This also reminds me of a story from a friend who felt it was not that important to have a password on her phone. After all, she said, it is too inconvenient and "*I don't have anything private on it.*" (*If only I had a dollar for all the times I hear this excuse*).

It all started when she lost her purse one day while out shopping. Within her purse were two things you would expect to find: her wallet and phone. When the crook started looking through her phone, he noticed an entry in the contact list (*and frequently called number*) to "*Hubby*". He proceeded to send a text message to "*Hubby*" complaining about forgetting their PIN number and needing to withdraw some cash at the ATM. Seeing this call for help from "*supposedly*" his wife, he promptly replied with the PIN number for their joint account. The crook, armed with not only the PIN but also the bankcard, proceeded to withdraw money up to the daily limit.

Do you see the problem? She had no phone, so she could not tell her husband she had lost her purse. He sees a text from a "*known*" person and responds with personal information. A phone passcode could have prevented this little fiasco.

NOTE: *it is also important to remember NEVER to disclose personal info via email or text, especially financial data. In this case, a quick phone call instead to his wife would have also prevented disaster.*

You've Got Mail

Email has become a mission-critical part of so many people's lives. This is beyond the corporate environment. Even my wife approaches a point of panic if her email becomes unavailable. The reality is that email has become an integral part of our society. This gives us simplicity and timeliness in many tasks, but it also leads to several concerns. In this chapter, we will cover some of the things we can do to improve our email experience and start controlling our email, rather than allowing it to control us.

Email Hoaxes and Frauds

One of the most frustrating things to me in my career as an IT professional is email. Moreover, nothing in email is as frustrating as the constant flood of hoaxes and frauds passed around daily. This garbage, along with spam, is the reason we hear consistent estimates that 90%+ of the email floating around is unsolicited trash. It wastes our time, takes up space, and causes us to have to spend a lot of money just to try to keep it out of our inboxes. On top of that, we also have the added risk of malicious software creeping into our computers because of the email garbage.

In this book, we will explore the problems created by hoaxes and frauds. The problems created are much bigger than some people may realize. It is also easy to put a stop to most of it with very simple, and free, actions. (*For more information also refer to my other book, "Don't Throw IT ~ Get to Know IT", where we dig much deeper into the malicious software types.*) Let us expose a few of the most common hoaxes right now:

- No company will give away a gift certificate or merchandise in return for you forwarding an email.

- Forwarding of an email will not result in donations to sick or injured children, eternal salvation, or in you becoming instantly rich and famous.

- You cannot track emails for marketing purposes.

- No reputable company needs your username, password, PIN, or other identifying information to "*verify*" your account.

- Nobody notifies Lottery winners via email, no matter the country of origin.

- People in foreign countries are not legitimately looking for strangers to import millions of dollars.

- Forwarding an email message will not cause anything special to happen on your computer.

- The IRS or the FBI will not contact you via email...they prefer a more "*direct*" approach.

If you laughed a little as you read those bullet points, you have obviously been the recipient of a few hoaxes. These are profound time wasters, and cost IT shops the world over millions in trying to keep them from clogging up systems. Add to that the amount of time IT professionals have to spend explaining to users why a lawyer is not really transferring them $10 million from a long-lost uncle in exchange for their bank account number and you begin to see the cost of the email and Internet hoax.

Have you ever wondered what may be a telltale sign of a hoax in your inbox? While it can take on many forms, a hoax nowadays seems to follow a few common threads. Here are a few things that should make your hoax radar start beeping wildly:

- If an item is marked URGENT, IMPORTANT, or states THIS IS NOT A JOKE! Usually this is someone trying a little too hard to convince you of something. A lot of exclamation points and all-capital letters is a good sign of hoax potential.

- A warning to *"Tell All Your Friends"*. This is typically an attempt to get you to forward it on and perpetuate the hoax.

- When it states, *"This is NOT a Hoax"*, I find that it typically is a hoax. I especially tire of the ones what include a statement that their brother's uncle's nephew's cousin's sister works at Microsoft® and knows this is a fact. Reputable companies do not issue alerts through their employees. They utilize press releases and other official channels.

- If the message warns of a consequence for not taking an action, I remind myself that my action or inaction in an email is not the end of the world!

68

- If the message is from a business you do not do business with, especially banks, then it is definitely a hoax.

- If you receive a message with a lot of entries below indicating it has been forwarded multiple times (*usually you will see dozens of previous peoples email addresses as you scroll down*) you can just about hang your hat on the fact that you are dealing with a chain letter. (*At a minimum, you know you are dealing with a sender that did not take time to follow good email etiquette. More on this later in the chapter.*)

Verifying Legitimacy

Checking the legitimacy of an email or Internet item has gotten much easier over the years. There are reputable sites on the Internet where you can plug in some of the highlights of the message and check its validity. I find myself doing this quite a bit every time I scan through my Facebook newsfeed. Some of the sites I use are:

- **www.SNOPES.com**

- **www.HOAXBUSTERS.org**

- **www.FACECROOKS.com**

- **www.HOAX-SLAYER.com**

- **www.SCAMBUSTERS.org**

- **www.TRUTHORFICTION.com**

Have you ever wondered why people create and distribute these hoaxes and frauds? The simplest, and most accurate, answer may be that people just simply like to start rumors. It is not too different from when each of us was on the playground in elementary school. With the Internet age, our playground now extends worldwide. Moreover, you can imagine how huge it can grow…and how fast. Just think of this: If you forward a message to ten people and they each forward it on to ten people….and this continues a few more times…you can quickly get to the millions of emails being sent in a relatively short period of time.

What about the emails purportedly for charity, or for helping to locate missing children? These CAN be legitimate, though many times are erroneous or out of date. Your best course of action if you seriously want to help will be to contact the actual charity or authority and offer assistance directly. It is an unfortunate side effect of the hoax that it can, and does damage the reputation of otherwise legitimate charities and causes. It is unfortunate that you cannot trust everything you see or read on the Internet or in your email. Do not add to the problem by continuing to pass on the rubbish.

∞ ∞ ∞ ∞ ∞

"My computer could be more encouraging.
You know, instead of "invalid password",
why not something like,
"Ooooh, you're so close!"?"
~ Lisa Porter

∞ ∞ ∞ ∞ ∞

Address Forging

It happens all too often: you receive an email that appears to be from a friend, you open it up, and now you find your computer slowed to a crawl due to malicious software entering your system. Unfortunately, just because an email appears to be from someone does not mean that person really sent it. It is a phenomenon called email spoofing, or email forging. Think of it this way: When you send a letter, what stops you from putting someone else's name and address on the return address section?

Email forging does not only involve pretending to be your friend or co-worker. Phishing is a common issue that results from email forging. In a phishing attempt, a malicious person attempts to trick someone into giving up information one would not normally disclose. Phishing attacks typically appear to be from your financial institutions, as the bad person wants to gain access to money for a quick financial gain. By pretending to be your bank, they hope to get you to fall for their ruse. Sneaky, huh?

How do you know if the email is legitimate before you open it up? There is no telltale way of saying if an email is legitimate or not, just as there is no way to verify the sender of a letter in your mailbox. While most "*traditional*" advice states to only open email you are expecting to receive...it is not realistic advice. Unlike monthly bills and periodicals, we cannot truly predict what email we will receive. You never truly know when Uncle Charlie will send you the latest and greatest joke making its rounds across the Internet.

While there is no guaranteed method to verify the legitimacy of an email, paying attention to what you see can minimize the potential of opening a malicious message. You have little information to evaluate against, and knowing what is *"normal"* for your email will help in this endeavor.

- Pay attention to the SUBJECT.

- Take note of the sender.

- Were you expecting the email?

Pay attention to the subject. Many malicious email messages will have strange, misspelled, or otherwise out of the ordinary subject lines. Seeing things like all caps or strange wording typically indicate spam messages. It is important to note that many Spammers today will begin their subject with *"RE:"* in an attempt to make you think they are replying to something you sent them earlier.

Take note of the sender. If the sender is not a person or business you hear from, it may cause you to pay extra attention. The more obvious issue is the email from the bank or business that you do not do business with currently, or past. I do not understand why people open email from a bank they do not even do business with in the first place!

Were you expecting the message? While you cannot predict your messages that does not mean you should open everything. If you receive an unexpected email, there is no rule that says you cannot delete it. If it is truly important, the sender will get back in touch with you. Besides, the world will not end if you miss a joke or two.

Examining the legitimacy of the email does not end once you open the email. You still need to pay attention to the contents, especially when the email is in regards to a personal account such as with your business or banking institution.

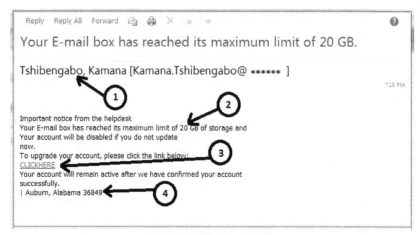

Sample Phishing Email

In the sample phishing email, we can see a few things to give us an indication that it is not authentic. I will describe the steps I would apply to evaluate the message:

1. The sender of this message is unknown. I would not trust a notice from someone I do not know or recognize. When in doubt, you should verify their information. No legitimate business should fault you for checking and being safe. HOWEVER, do not use contact information contained in the email…use business contact information from a trusted source like a bill or statement.

2. Be aware of the policies and rules regarding email, especially with your work account. In this example, I realized the incorrect information on exceeding my limits, which contradicted my company's policy. Awareness of the policies where you do business, whether it is at your job or with your email provider can prevent quite a bit of problems.

3. NEVER follow a link within an email message. It is as easy to fake an email address, as it is to falsify a link to a website. I do not follow links in email messages even when I am sure they are from authentic sources. The danger is simply too great.

4. This message indicates plainly that it is from Auburn, Alabama. I work in the state of Mississippi, and our company has no facilities in Auburn, so this is obviously a fake. We had a case in our office where users fell for a fake email that was from Iowa! Simply paying attention can do wonders in preventing malicious infections.

Following the link in this sample message would take you to a page requesting your username and password. Once entered the page would thank you and advise your email limit has expanded. In reality, the hacker would then use your credentials to send hundreds of thousands of email messages from their account to people all over the world, infecting machines and causing quite a headache. How do I know? Because we actually had a user in a past job fall for this and shut down our email systems until we could recover and have our business removed from bad email lists all over the world. It took days to recover.

∞ ∞ ∞ ∞ ∞
"Technology makes it possible for people to
gain control over everything, except over technology."
~ John Tudor
∞ ∞ ∞ ∞ ∞

I Did Not Send This Person An Email!

Have you ever received email delivery failure notices from people you never sent an email to in the first place? When you start receiving these notices, we call the messages "*backscatter*". Authors of spam and viruses wish to make their messages appear to originate from a legitimate source to fool recipients into opening the message. They use web-crawling software to scan web comments, message boards, and web pages for legitimate email addresses. They can also gain your address following an infection on a friend or co-worker's computer, stealing your information from their address book. The "*bad guy*" can then pretend to be you (*called "spoofing"*) and send random messages in bulk to sometimes thousands of e-mail addresses. When this happens, you end up receiving multiple delivery failure notices.

The safest action to take with this type of junk is to delete the message. While it would be wonderful to tell you there is some magic button or program we can use to stop the junk, it is simply not the case. Most email scanners do quite a bit to reduce this sort of junk, but even the best systems are unable to stop it fully. These replies you are receiving are legitimate messages, and to stop them all would stop you from receiving legitimate messages you need regarding e-mails you actually send.

RANDOM TECH TIP:

Did you know the placement of your wireless router in your home can affect how well your wireless performs? You should avoid setting it close to metal surfaces, such as file cabinets or desks. You should also attempt to locate it as centrally as possible, as the signals tend to radiant in a circle.

✝ ✝ ✝ ✝ ✝

Disposable Email Accounts

What do I mean by a disposable email address? Many people are not aware that such things actually exist. Luckily, they do and they are very helpful in the right situation. A disposable email address will be active for a limited amount of time. This period is typically only 10-20 minutes. I have listed a few of the more common disposable email address providers below. Please be aware that these services can change from time to time, so between me writing this section and you reading this section there could be changes:

- **www.GUERRILLAMAIL.com**; good for 60 minutes

- **www.GETAIRMAIL.com**; good for 24 hours

Why would people want to use a disposable email address? When you sign up for some things such as a coupon for the restaurant you want to visit tonight, or when you go to read an article and they insist you provide an email address to continue, if you provide your real email address you will start seeing an enormous increase in spam email you will receive.

Did I just say that signing up for coupons or reading news articles can lead to your inbox filling up with spam? Yes, I did. Email marketing is a big business. Every time you give someone your email address, you run the risk of them selling that address to countless companies who will flood your inbox with ads and offers. An ever-growing issue, spam will not go away anytime soon.

∞ ∞ ∞ ∞ ∞

"Computers have lots of memory but no imagination."
~ Author Unknown

∞ ∞ ∞ ∞ ∞

Multiple Email Addresses

Another tool many people use to help organize their inbox is multiple email accounts to manage and separate online correspondence. I personally utilize this method to manage my email. With the availability of free email accounts from providers such as Google®, Yahoo®, and Microsoft®, this is a very easy management tool to implement. It is even easy to maneuver multiple accounts, as we will soon illustrate.

First, we need to define how we want to divide and categorize our email. I will use myself as an example, though your own methods for organizing email may very well differ. All of our minds work differently...and if yours works like mine...I truly feel sorry for those who are close to and love you! ☺ I have a few specific high-level categories I first assign to my email messages. I then use the email address associated with these categories when performing certain actions:

- One account for family and friends

- One account for business correspondence

- One account for my "*day*" job (*i.e. the office*)

- One account for online gaming (X-Box)

- One account for junk

Does this seem like a lot to keep up with effectively? It is actually easier than you think. Providers build modern email systems to handle multiple accounts with ease. A little planning up front and you will find it very easy, and a welcome tool in keeping garbage out of your way when you turn on your email client. I will cover a few of the more popular options to demonstrate ways to optimize the use of these multiple accounts. Your actual solution may vary slightly, though the principle will be the same.

Managing Multiple Accounts Online

Let us look at Google's Gmail, the online service I personally use as an example. Though you may choose a different provider, the general steps and considerations should be the same. It is simply not possible for me to show every scenario and solution for you in these pages. (*The numbered points on the next page refer to the illustration*)

RANDOM TECH TIP:

Have you seen those Facebook posts where people proclaim no one can use their images, etc. without their permission? Bad news...by agreeing to use social media services you agree to allow them to use your information for advertising services and such. That is why it is important that you READ before you agree to terms and conditions. A post on your news feed will not provide any alteration to what you have already agreed to legally.

✝ ✝ ✝ ✝ ✝

Example of Multiple Email Setup Online

1. In this area, you can add multiple accounts to send from different addresses. When you have multiple accounts added, you can choose the account to use when sending an email by selecting the TO: portion of your email. This will allow you to send from any of your accounts.

2. This section refers to how you reply to a message. For most people, the best option would be to reply from the account that received the email. For example, if you receive an email at **WORK@mail.com** you would want your replies to use that same address. You would not want to reply from your **PLAY@mail.com** account.

3. This section is where you would add your assorted accounts. In this example, Gmail will reach out to each of your accounts regularly and check your mail for you. This will allow you to manage all emails under one account.

Managing Multiple Accounts within a Program

For this example, I will use Microsoft® Outlook. This should be similar to any client you are using on your home or office computer. Again, it is simply not possible for me to show an example for each possible program, though the settings will be similar. As you would expect with a Microsoft® product like Outlook you can expect to use something called a wizard to add multiple accounts. A wizard is simply a guided set of steps to accomplish the task...in this case, adding a new account. Most other email clients will use a similar process, making the procedure simple.

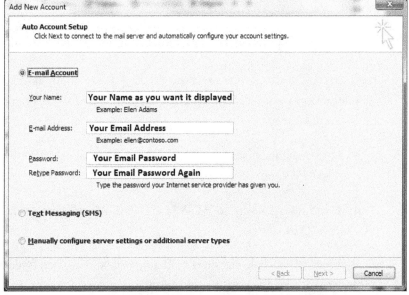

Example Wizard Screen to Add Email Accounts

Adding your email accounts is an easy process. We will likely want to take a few more steps to subdivide our messages once they make it to the email inbox. You can accomplish this in Outlook (*or your selected client*) by setting rules on how you want Outlook to handle your messages. (*Instructions for creating rules will follow shortly.*) I use automatic email rules to manage where email I receive will go based on different criteria. This helps me to sort email based on its importance. Where my business or personal email may go into a folder I check often, I would allow my junk email to go into a less important folder that I may only check periodically to make sure there were no items requiring attention. You can organize your email according to your own preferred priorities!

Folders are truly the solution to managing multiple accounts and keeping information organized. I do not try to get TOO fancy with the rules either. An example of mine are:

- Move messages sent to **WORK@email.com** to the folder "*Work Messages*"

- Move messages sent to **PERSONAL@email.com** to the folder "*Personal Messages*"

- Move messages sent to **NEWSLETTER@email.com** to the folder "*Newsletters*"

By keeping it simple and clear I am able to deal with each folder as appropriate without having to wade through a sea of garbage and distractions. If only we could deal with the morning commute traffic so easily!

Setting up a rule for managing the flow of email is simple. The wizard will guide you through the steps, though I will briefly outline the process below:

- From within your email program locate the *"Rules"* link. In Outlook, this is typically on the top bar. If using an online service this will be under *"Settings"*

- Define the condition(s) that will trigger the rule. This will typically be if it is received into a certain account, from a particular sender, or has a subject containing specific words or phrases

- Select the action(s) you want the program to take once it meets those conditions. This could involve moving the message to a specific folder, deleting it, flagging it as important, or many other options depending on the software used

Result After Completing Rule Wizard:

Step 3: Review rule description (click an underlined value to edit)

Apply this rule after the message arrives
sent to knowit@techknolutions.com
move it to the BOOK E-Mail folder
and stop processing more rules

Example Results from Rules Setup in Microsoft® Outlook

Email Etiquette

Writing etiquette is becoming a lost art. In the world of email and text messages, there has been less focus on etiquette and more focus on developing a shorthand method to convey messages. It is for this reason that I make students in my college computer courses complete tests that require complete sentences and paragraphs. It is not that I am trying to take the place of the English teachers. It is simply that I want them to remember that even with email and text messaging it is still important to communicate effectively and professionally. This need is very evident in email correspondence. I have identified a few areas we need to be mindful of when formulating an email to friends, family, co-workers, and even strangers.

- Do not add recipient addresses until last.

- Do not write angrily.

- Beware of *"Reply All"*.

- Use sentence case.

- Use CC and BCC properly.

- Do not use email for private communication.

- Use a meaningful subject.

- Re-read before sending.

- Mind your attachments.

- Do not forward junk mail, hoaxes, or jokes.

- Keep it brief and to the point.

- Do not try to *"cutesy"* it up.

- Return receipts can be bad.

- Clean up your forwards and replies.

- When in doubt, pick up the phone.

Do not add recipient addresses until last. I placed this item first because I see so many times where this simple act can save so much unnecessary heartache. By waiting until the end to address your message you can take a few minutes and review before hitting the "*Send*" button. It is so automatic to some people to send before taking a few extra breaths. Makes me wonder how many friendships and relationships an itchy "*Send*" finger has affected.

Do not write angrily. Writing while emotionally charged may make you say things you cannot take back. Putting angry feelings in writing makes the potential for damage even greater. Check your emotions before your fingers hit the keyboard. A lot of venom can flow from your fingertips, and once you put it in writing, it is a permanent record of a temporary emotion.

Beware of "Reply All". You do not need to tell everything to everyone. Evaluate your message before you reply to everyone. It could be that your response only needs to go to one or two of the original recipients. I cannot begin to count the number of email replies I continue to receive when I am many levels away from the initial need for my involvement. Do not be afraid to manage the list of recipients and do your part to reduce needless wasting of time for people no longer needed in the conversation.

Use sentence case. This means capitalizing the first word of your sentence as well as those other proper words requiring capitalization. When you CAPITALIZE all of the words in a message, it is the equivalent of SHOUTING at your recipient. If you do not follow at least the basic principles of capitalization, it makes your writing look sloppy and the recipient feels unworthy of your taking a little extra effort.

Use CC and BCC properly. These two fields are commonly misused. You should use CC (*Carbon Copy*) when you need to copy someone to keep them in the loop on the information, but it may not be necessary for them to reply. BCC (*Blind Carbon Copy*) does the same, though each recipient of the email will not see anyone else listed in the BCC field. The BCC field is also a great place to list everyone when you are sending an email such as an invitation to a large group of people. This will keep from exposing everyone's email addresses to everyone else and keep the message looking neat. However, you should NEVER use the BCC field as a way to talk behind someone's back. Pay attention to the next paragraph if you wonder why.

Do not use email for private communication. If you are not willing to put the information on the nightly news, do not place it in an email. Sending an email is the equivalent of your endorsement on an idea, and it can come back to haunt you! Imagine how many celebrities would have benefited from this simple advice. The reality is that when you send an email it is the digital equivalent of sending a postcard. It is easy to misuse by others by other with malicious intent. Another thing to consider for those who send jokes and messages via email: If any of your recipients forward your message, your name could remain attached to the original message. I have seen cases when this has come back to bite people professionally and created a "*resume-altering*" experience.

Use a meaningful subject. The subject line lets your recipient know what the email is about, along with letting a skeptical recipient know if it is worth opening in the first place. Your subject should accurately reflect the topic of your email. A good subject can be the difference between the recipients reading your email, deleting it into cyberspace without even a glance, or sending it to the SPAM junk pile.

Re-read before sending. This is a good practice no matter the medium. Do not trust that what you thought in your head is what actually flowed out on the keyboard. The little bit of time needed to re-read through your latest email is worth a ton of embarrassment later in the event it says something other than what you meant it to say.

Mind your attachments. Before you add an attachment to your email, you need to be mindful of what you are attaching and what effect it may have on your recipient. When attaching items to an email the biggest mistake I see people make is regarding the size of items they try to attach. The truth is the intention of email was not to transfer large items across the Internet. There are other tools created for that task. As a result, many email systems will automatically reject an email containing too large of attachments. How large is too large? In many cases, systems may reject messages that exceeds 10 Megabytes (*10 MB*) in size. Even if systems allow larger attachments, it is inconsiderate to do so as it can negatively affect storage and performance. It is important to note that Megabytes come AFTER Kilobytes (KB), so if your email attachment ends in KB you are OK. It is when the letters behind that number change to MB you need to be concerned. If you see GB (*Gigabyte*) then it is a definite no-no! When you find yourself needing to send larger items, consider the cloud collaboration options from the earlier chapter.

Do not forward junk mail, hoaxes, or jokes. Many of us know that feeling when you receive an email from the relative that forwards every piece of junk mail. Do not be that person. The flood of misinformation drifting through email systems worldwide waste time for recipients while causing unnecessary clutter inside their inboxes. Users who consistently pass on unwanted information also create *"the boy who cried wolf"* syndrome for recipients: when you do forward a legitimate message, people may ignore it thinking it is more junk mail.

Keep it brief and to the point. Nothing turns off a reader like a long and drawn out message. Try to sum it up in as few sentences as possible. There are numerous studies floating around that point to low attention spans when reading email. The bottom line is to make your point clearly and move on. There is no need to drag it out with colorful language. *This same "Keep It Brief" advice also applies to text messaging on your phone!*

Do not try to "cutesy" it up. Fancy fonts and colored backgrounds do not add to your email. In fact, they tend to take away from the readability and credibility of your message. While teenagers may employ these tactics, I would advise most adults to avoid these undertakings. When it comes to business correspondence, it becomes even more important to avoid anything viewed as unprofessional. This is especially true if you are trying to make a first impression with a prospective employee or client.

Return receipts can be bad. As some of you may know, you can request a return receipt when you send a message to someone. This will attempt to get the receiving system to send you a reply when the recipient receives and/or opens your message. I use the term "*attempt*" because many systems reject these requests.

Personally, I do NOT recommend people respond to, or even request, read receipts when dealing with email. Besides the extra traffic and clutter these read receipts create in your inbox as well as throughout email systems, responding to these read receipts can result in you receiving even MORE junk mail! How, you ask?

- A junk email comes in from **WhoZaMaWhatzIT.com**

- Along with the junk mail is a read receipt request.

- Your computer automatically responds that you received the junk mail.

- The junk mail sender now knows that your email address is valid and can send you even more junk mail.

- Just because a message is *"received"* does not mean the recipient read it.

Clean up your forwards and replies. Have you ever received an email only to have to scroll through pages and pages of names from previous forwarding? You know the one…where you have to scroll down 12 pages before you get to whatever joke the sender wanted you to see. If you truly cannot resist forwarding the latest viral joke, or even if it is a legitimate business correspondence, take the extra few seconds to delete the unnecessary information from the message. This is as simple as selecting the unneeded information in the message (*like the addresses of all previous recipients*) and deleting them, leaving only the needed information to send. Trust me…your recipient(s) will appreciate you!

When in doubt, pick up the phone. Face it folks…while email is wonderful for general conversation, there is still a time and place for the good, old-fashioned telephone call. When you receive an email pay attention before you take action. If you doubt the validity, and especially if it deals with financial or other personal information, pick up the phone and call to check it out. Even then, beware…use a number you know is correct! In the digital age it is extremely simple, and common, to include false information, especially in an email or on the Internet. A past bill or the back of your credit card are a great source for legitimate contact information.

Managing Your Email
This section dedicated to my wonderful mother-in-law.

When you look through your email inbox, what do you see? If you see a bunch of old and outdated articles of junk mail then chances are you do not regularly manage your email. I know this may come as a shock to many of you, but the sales ad from a year ago is no longer valid! I wonder at times if it would help to start a special multi-step program to let people know it really is OK to delete email. Too many people subscribe to the *"I'll read it later"* mentality. This ends up leaving hundreds or thousands of email messages lingering in your inbox making it nearly impossible to find the messages you really do need.

Do yourself a favor…if you have already read it, are not going to act on it, and especially if it refers to an item long expired…delete it! No matter how much you beg and plead, the store will not honor last year's sale prices on that must have item!

Backing It Up

∞ ∞ ∞ ∞ ∞

"Most computer users don't think about backing up their software until the day they lose it."

~Don Rittner

∞ ∞ ∞ ∞ ∞

I touched briefly on backups in my first book, "*Don't Throw IT ~ Get To Know IT*", but it bears repeating, along with its own chapter, here. Unfortunately, I have found that people begin to think about backing up AFTER they experience a problem. This can be an expensive mistake which is easy, and relatively inexpensive, to avoid. In this chapter, we will explore what we should be backing up, along with discovering the most efficient ways to protect your data.

We must also remember an additional important aspect of backing up as well: backups are not just for protection from system failure or loss. Backups also enable you to move your information from an older computer to a newer one. Many of us have likely been through the migration between computers. Nothing is more frustrating in the process then to turn on your new computer and find a function or piece of information needed is missing.

Why Are Backups Important?

Being a computer nerd, I am faced all too often with examples of why backing up data is important. I could tell horror stories of people accidently losing valuable data. I have been involved in situations where carelessness has resulted in loss of valuable business information. I have seen where a disgruntled employee decided to delete their files and email before walking out the door. I have heard the horrors of crashing computers as the hard drive fails and literally "*grinds*" the user's data, in a noise that can only be compared to the sound of a hundred fingernails running down a chalkboard. (*For the younger readers, a chalkboard was an item teachers wrote on before the age of dry-erase and PowerPoint*)

You can imagine that after confronting the things that can go wrong with digital data I am always surprised by the level of apathy I witness when I ask someone if they back up their computer's data. I often feel like the cop pulling over a speeder, as I can just about predict the excuses:

- Backing up? Is that like putting my computer in reverse?

- I do not really have anything important on my computer.

- My computer is too new to worry about backing up.

- Backing up is too difficult.

- I do not know how to back up my computer.

DISCLAIMER:
There is a group of people that
do NOT ponder these questions:
Those who have experienced data loss
because of system failure or loss.

Backing up? Is that like putting my computer in reverse? I guess the first thing we really need to address is to explain what it means to back up your computer. To back up your computer means to store your information in a place OTHER THAN your computer. This will therefore enable you to get your information back if something were to happen to your computer.

Would you like an example? The most important data I deal with would have to be my family's digital pictures. These cover everything since my kids were born. If something to happen to them I am sure I would no longer be able to sleep with BOTH eyes closed...and my couch is not THAT comfortable! For those reasons, along with the fact I truly cherish the memories those pictures represent, I ensure they are stored in more than one place...a key element in backing up your data. We will discuss the importance of distance with your data later in this chapter.

I do not really have anything important on my computer. This particular excuse is a computer nerd's kryptonite. When heard it literally brings us to our knees in frustration. Are you shaking your head in disbelief wondering why I would say such a thing? I imagine the way I feel when I hear this excuse is the same as the police officer when they hear someone state they did not realize they were speeding. Ignorance of your data is no excuse!

Even someone using their computer a few hours fresh out of the box has likely already accumulated data that would benefit from a backup. I will cover this in detail when we discuss what to back up later in this chapter, but just to get your mind thinking ahead, consider these items now:

- Pictures and documents

- Internet favorite links

- Music and video files

- Smartphone/Tablet synchronized information

- Email account configurations and messages

- Programs and their settings/data

- The operating system itself

My computer is too new to worry about backing up. It is such a common misconception to think the age of technology is a representation of its reliability. Just as a new car fresh off the showroom floor can leave you stranded on the side of the road, your computer can let you down shortly after emerging from its box. We must not lose sight of the fact that these items are mass-produced and problems can occur.

Besides the possibility of an issue from the manufacturer, that giant pothole you hit in the road while leaving the store could have caused issues deep inside that can surface when you least expect it. You would not dare leave the car dealership without insurance, and you should think of your data with the same care and concern. After all, backing up is, in fact, insurance against loss.

Backing up is too difficult. While in the past this may have been more applicable, backing up your data nowadays is almost as simple as putting gas in your car. The products available to the home and office user to conduct reliable backing up of information have become increasingly simple to use. While my co-workers at the data center may use words OTHER THAN simple when they are backing up terabytes of data, the ease provided to the home and small office user to perform this essential task to protect their data are painless and require no advanced degree in *"nerd-ology."*

I do not know how to back up my computer. Refer to the previous paragraph. We all know that when something is cumbersome and difficult, the chances of performance become rare. However, with advances in technology the backing up process has become a model of simplicity in the chaos of the digital era. We will discuss these simple methods later in this chapter, including the use of cloud services and externally connected devices that are readily accessible to all, including the novices of the world.

What to Back Up

Now that I have you excited to get your computer backed up, and we have dispelled the common excuses presented by those that overlook the backup process, we get to the million-dollar question of WHAT we should back up in order to be effective. As with most questions when it comes to technology, your answers may vary. No matter the details; however, it still comes down to one basic question: *What information can you not live without having?* It could be pictures or videos of the kids and grandkids. It could be a term paper or essay. It could be links to your favorite sites. While the specific answer to this question may vary between us, the core result remains the same...no one wants to lose what they deem important.

Let us revisit that list from earlier in this chapter. You remember...the one we brushed when the answer was *"I don't have anything important on my computer."* I hope that your mind has been buzzing since reading it and you now have a mental list of things that may be important after all. Just in case, let us look at it again:

- Pictures and documents

- Internet favorite links

- Music and video files

- Smartphone synchronized information

- Email account configurations and messages

- Programs and their settings/data

- The operating system itself

While definitely not all-inclusive, we can probably agree this list covers a bulk of your important information. Depending on your computer activities, you may even have a database, tax information, or other items scattered throughout your computer that would result in a significant need for antacid medicine if they were lost.

Pictures and documents. I mentioned earlier that I worry most about losing the pictures on my computer. As such, they are a huge consideration in my backup process. Likewise, I would hate to lose the documents I have been working on, such as this book and a couple of others that are in their infancy. Do you have similar, important items worth saving on your computer?

Internet favorite links. Often overlooked, web site shortcuts become very important when misplaced. Over time, most users visit plenty of sites that you have marked as a "*favorite*" and you expect to be able to return without having to recall the exact Internet address. If you perform work from home, this list can become even more vital. Making sure you can restore these can be just as important as the essay you have been working on for months.

Music and video files. Long gone are the days of albums, 8-tracks, cassettes, and even CD's. More and more music is being bought and sold digitally, placing these valuable files on your computer. They likely consume a good portion of space, and their loss would be frustrating. If the music files in question happen to belong to a teenager, they may even categorize their loss as tragic. In addition, video is following closely in the music footsteps, especially when one considers video of their child's first steps or a dance recital.

Smartphone/Tablet synchronized information. We must face a digital reality…Smartphones and Tablets have become as important to some people as their arm. We all are likely now thinking of someone who has one of these devices, seemingly surgically attached, to their hands or ear. In fact, I bet you are smiling thinking of them right now…or is it YOU?

Email account configurations and messages. If you were watching *"Family Feud"* on television and they asked the question: *"Of One-Billion people surveyed, what would they consider the most important function of their computer?"* I would be willing to bet your next paycheck the number one answer would be email. In fact, nothing at my day job as a network manager causes more anxiety and chaos than the thought of losing email services. While some of you may only check your email online, relying on the email provider in the cloud to keep things backed up, a growing majority of folks likely uses a program like Outlook or Thunderbird to pull email into your computer to manage it locally.

∞ ∞ ∞ ∞ ∞
What is Thunderbird, you ask?
Similar to Outlook,
it is a free application to manage
your email locally quickly and easily.
(http://www.mozilla.org/en-US/thunderbird/)
∞ ∞ ∞ ∞ ∞

Programs and their settings/data. So often, the user overlooks the data stored inside programs. While in the overall scheme of things this may not apply to everyone, for those to whom it does apply, the loss of this data could be devastating. For example, if you play games on your computer, the files that record your progress are significant. On the other hand, if you do your taxes with your computer, it would be that information. To evaluate this question you would need to look through your computer and identify the programs you have installed and use to perform your daily functions.

The operating system itself. By a show of hands, who reading this book would be comfortable reinstalling their operating system (*i.e. Windows, Mac OS, or Linux*) from scratch onto nothing but a blank hard drive? If you are now raising your hand, you are in the minority of users. (*I see you...you can put your hand down now.*) For most people this would be a daunting task, and someone with inexperience should definitely not tackle it. Luckily, the backup process can address this as well. We will discuss this in detail in a later segment.

Once you have identified and answered the question of WHAT you want or need to back up, you are prepared to move on to the next portion of effectively backing up your computer. This next stage is taking action to do it, and we will cover that next.

How to Back Up

Luckily, backing up has become a simple undertaking. Long gone are the cumbersome procedures of the past. Of all the methods out there, for the average user two methods float to the top for their effectiveness, simplicity, and reputation for being reliable. There are other methods, such as using CD's, DVD's, and USB thumb drives. (*Due to the space limitations and cumbersome nature of these smaller devices, we will not cover them in this book.*) In the interest of simplicity and applicability to all readers (*and operating systems*), I will focus on the two that have universal appeal, which are:

- External hard drives

- Cloud backup solutions

External hard drives. Typically connected to your computer via USB cable, they contain software from the manufacturer that monitors your computer for changes and makes a copy of your files to the unit. These devices really are simple and effective for the money. Simply put, when my wife downloads pictures from her camera, the program is smart enough to see the changes and immediately copies these new pictures to the backup device.

Another added benefit of the external drive is *"versioning"* control. Have you ever been working on a document only to wish you could go back to a previous edition? As I have been writing this book I have encountered that situation several times. With versioning the backup device will not only have a current copy of your file, but will also be able to save the previous few copies before changes making this as easy as a couple clicks.

I am a huge fan of utilizing the external drive for backing up my computers. It is important to note that while this does a wonderful job of protecting you from a failure on your computer, the external drive is still susceptible to loss from catastrophic events such as fire or storms, as well as theft. For this reason, you should consider a layered approach to backup and use a cloud provider, discussed below.

Cloud backup solutions. There are quite a few providers for reliable cloud backup solutions, such as my current solution, Carbonite® (**www.CARBONITE.com**). They provide additional features making them an ideal choice when backing up your computer. Similar to the external drive option above, the cloud backup provider will also place a small software program on your computer to monitor for file changes. Once it detects files changes, it will copy the new file to the providers cloud system for you automatically. Settings will also allow you to retain previous versions so that you can go back to previous edits as needed.

Cloud backups rely on your Internet connection and speed to be effective. This can sometimes cause some concern for many users, as home upload speeds can be considerably slow depending on your provider. This is primarily an issue when you are first setting up the program, as that is when you upload the bulk of your data. It is not uncommon to hear reports of initial uploads taking several weeks. The good news is that once this completes future updates take considerably less time, as it only needs to transfer information added or changed. This is all dependent on the amount of data you have and the speed of your Internet provider, so results will vary.

Besides having your data safely stored off-premise, another beneficial side effect of the online backup is that most provers will allow you to log into their website to access backed up files. This can be rather convenient when you need to get to a file or picture while away from your home computer.

Mobile Device Backups

Make sure you also regularly backup your mobile devices, such as smart phones and tablets. These devices continue to be a major part of our lives. Like your computer, they can fall victim to breakage or theft so they need your attention too. With the popularity of using these devices for pictures and video, they can contain rather valuable memories for families.

Backing up these devices is generally a simple and automated process. The actual steps will be dependent on your device and available from the manufacturer, such as Apple, Android, or Amazon. It is typically as simple as plugging the device into your computer and allowing the manufacturer's program to take over the backup procedure. Another option, which is increasingly popular today, is automated backup to the provider's cloud storage services.

∞ ∞ ∞ ∞ ∞

Be aware that the cloud option COULD
come with a price tag,
especially if dealing
with photos and videos.
They tend to take up quite a bit of space.

∞ ∞ ∞ ∞ ∞

Securing Your Backup

We have stressed the importance of creating a backup of your data to protect against loss. A backup plan is not truly complete unless you also consider the security of your information. Your backups could contain passwords, tax information, and other personal items best kept under your control. The previously mentioned solutions provide methods for securing backed up data, typically through implementation of a secure password. It is important to utilize these tools. Do not think of the password as an inconvenience. Instead, view them as a way of protecting you and your family from the heartache and headache of identity theft (*which we will discuss in the next chapter*). If you read my other book (*Don't Throw IT, Get To Know IT*) you will recall us talking about effective password protection using pass phrases. For those who have not yet read that wonderful work of literature (*what is your excuse...you really should check it out!*) I will put a tidbit of the password section here for you:

"When most think of a password, they instantly think of a dictionary style of word: Puppies, Kittens, Monkey, etc. What I would like you to do is expand beyond the word and think instead of a phrase. With a passphrase, you open up the complexity while also increasing the ability to remember. Can we really make it longer, more complex, AND easier to remember? The answer is a most definite yes!

A passphrase can be a series of words which you can string together to make more complex, all while simply repeating them in your head to remember. Confused? Please do not be, dear reader. Many of us have sayings, lyrics, poems, or Bible verses running through our heads. The basic passphrase is simply making THOSE your password! For example, instead of "Password123", you could use "NewOrleansSaintsWhoDat!" While this may still appear as dictionary words, the length of the password, along with its run-on nature, make it much more difficult to compromise. This is therefore even more secure than even a random password, like "v68P7qv0", and a HECK of a lot easier to remember. Furthermore, any password you can remember without writing it down becomes that much more secure, in my opinion."

Last But Not Least....

Testing the results of your backups is an often-overlooked part of the backup process. An unsuspecting user has shed many tears reaching for their backup only to discover it is blank! Testing the backup success does not have to be difficult either. Depending on your method(s) of backup, simply attempt a restore of an item or program. I will usually move a file, such as a picture or song, to another location on my computer (*typically the desktop*) and then attempt to use my backup provider's software to restore that file to its original location. I can then verify the restored file without risking the original. A simple sample restore now can save you heartache later!

IdentiSafe

*"People are prone to taking mental shortcuts.
They may know that they shouldn't give out certain
information, but the fear of not being nice,
the fear of appearing ignorant, the fear of a perceived
authority figure – all these are triggers,
which can be used by a social engineer to convince
a person to override established security procedures."*
~Kevin Mitnick

Our digital environment can be a scary place. Many of us have experienced, or know someone who has experienced, identity theft. It can be a scary thing to open our bank account and see that where there was once a balance is now empty. This sad reality plays out all too often. Luckily, there is quite a bit we can do to prevent becoming a victim. In this chapter, we will discuss the identity theft threat and offer suggestions to reduce the giant target thieves have drawn on each of our backs. Privacy is important and it is surely worth protecting.

How Do They Do That?

Thieves have plenty of tools at their disposal to attack and steal your identity. The common goal of this theft is for financial gain. Identity and credit theft accounts for billions of dollars in losses in the United States alone. Even more frightening is the increase in the number of victims under the age of 18. Imagine applying for a student loan and finding out you are already thousands of dollars in debt.

There are several methods of identity theft we should be aware of today. These can be online campaigns such as phishing and pharming. Those are discussed more in-depth in *"Don't Throw IT ~ Get To Know IT"*, my other book. Here we will discuss several additional threats that particularly target our identities:

- Vishing

- Dumpster diving

- Shoulder surfing

- Medical identity theft

- Credit card skimming

Vishing. Now here is a new term. Vishing is the practice of using social engineering frauds over the telephone system to gain your personal and/or financial information. People seem to believe what they hear on a telephone, and that is what makes this so dangerous. Additionally, with the utilization of Internet-based phone systems such as VoIP (*Voice over Internet Protocol*) it is very difficult for law enforcement to track down the offenders. It is important to remember that it is also nearly impossible to verify where a caller is actually located when calling you.

Your best defense against this voice-based threat? DO NOT reveal your personal information over the phone, especially when you did not initiate the call. Even if you are dealing with a company you deal with regularly, such as your bank, make sure it is at a number YOU know for a fact belongs to the company. Like so many other things…if it does not feel right…hang up!

Dumpster diving. This nasty little trick is why I recommend you shred your trash. It is exactly what it sounds like…digging through someone's trash to discover information to use against them. This could be things like credit card statements, credit offers, or other personal documents. It could even be information from your job, school, or banker.

Dumpster diving is a real threat, though many seem to think people surely would not dig through trash to get information. It is also very simple to defeat with a simple crosscut shredder. More effective than a straight-cut shredder, a crosscut shredder takes the extra step of cutting the long vertical strips in to smaller pieces by performing a horizontal cut. This produces a confetti of paper, effectively impossible to reassemble.

When speaking of dumpster diving and crosscut shredders, I would like to throw a thought out for you to consider. Do not JUST shred items you think of first such as bank statements and credit offers. Consider shredding ALL your paper products (*OK, except for the newspaper*). A determined thief could use that seemingly meaningless information against you. I am reminded of a story I saw where a dumpster diver used a thank you note a business received from a vendor to compromise a vulnerability in their multi-million dollar business.

Shoulder surfing. Ever had that feeling as if someone was watching you? Maybe behind you at the ATM or in line at the grocery store. My friend Charlie would refer to this as people getting into his "*bubble*". A person peeking over your shoulder can be unnerving to say the least (*along with the fact that it creeps Charlie out*). This may be the simplest to avoid…maintain your space and pay attention to those around you that may be paying more attention to what you are doing than they should. That casual peek could be all they need to learn your PIN number for when they pick your pocket later.

Medical identity theft. Not as commonly talked about, this can be a rather nasty little surprise when your next insurance bill comes in. Imagine someone seeking medical services using your name instead of their own. It would not take much, really. If someone simply heard your name at a clinic, there would not be much difficulty for them to pass your name off as their own. While this may be nearly impossible at a small town clinic where everyone knows each other, with so many more large clinics, the chances of the receptionist knowing you are minimal.

This problem is why it is SO important to pay attention to those billing statements you receive from your insurance company. Look for charges for services you did not receive or even conditions you do not have. You should also insist on detailed billing for medical services to ensure accuracy. With increasing medical costs, this is becoming more of an issue, and your best defense is to be proactive and pay attention.

Credit card skimming. While most of the other methods listed involve social engineering, skimming is a technology-based threat. We will discuss this more in-depth later in this chapter.

Counter Surveillance

We have all done it: The attendant brings the check, you hand them your card, and they disappear for a moment or two. Most of the time it is a safe process and everyone is happy. Unfortunately, that is not always the case. No credit monitoring in the world will protect you from the few seconds it takes for someone to snag your credit or debit card information and pay their utility bill or buy some Christmas presents.

Am I saying that everyone who takes your card is out to rip you off? Far from it! However, what I am saying is that it DOES warrant protection. Moreover, your first, best, and most reliable defense is looking back at you every time you brush your hair in the mirror. Simply being aware that it can happen is a critical step toward protection.

What are some things YOU can do to defend yourself against this theft? The reality is that if you visit a restaurant or similar establishment you may lose sight of your credit or debit card. It is just a reality now. While it may be necessary, you can still minimize your risk:

- Do NOT write your PIN number on your card

- Take your receipts, especially the copy showing your name, as this will contain at least a part of your account number

- Check your charges as soon as possible. Most charges will appear in online records the same night you make them.

Do you want me to scare you a little more? Have you ever used an ATM at a bank? How about the card scanner at your local gas station? Thieves can even use these areas to steal your information…and the card never leaves your hands! If everything goes as we expect, we go along feeling safe and secure, or so we think.

We sometimes find a dangerous device known as a *"skimmer"* on ATM's and other credit card scanners. Criminals use it to syphon millions from unsuspecting consumers. These cleverly manufactured devices look just like the *"official"* card scanner itself. Moreover, to make it effective, they are even intelligent enough to pass your card info on through to the real scanner so you can complete the transaction. Do you think your card is useless without the PIN number? They have features (*miniature cameras*) built in to record your PIN number when you enter your number on the keypad.

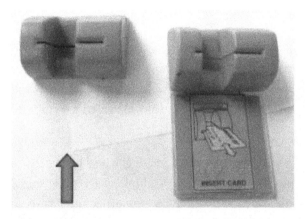

The real card reader slot.   The capture device

The side cut out is not visible when on the ATM.

With all these human and technological threats itching for a chance to grab your financial information, what in the world can we do to protect ourselves? We can minimize our risk by being aware:

- Look closely at the card reader BEFORE inserting your card

- Give the card reader a small tug to ensure it really IS real and attached to the machine

- Look for out of place objects like mirrors or cameras that may be trying to capture your PIN number

- If it does not "*feel*" right, do not do it!

Many times, if someone is going use your credit or debit card it will happen shortly after stealing. This is so they can commit their crime before you have a chance to report the loss. In many cases, they will also limit the charges to smaller purchases so as not to alert a credit card company or bank to unusual activity.

Recently a co-worker and I were visiting when he started to receive alerts related to his bank account. Multiple charges transpired in Dallas, Texas while we were sitting in my office in Flowood, Mississippi. Upon seeing the alerts, he immediately contacted his bank, following the call up with a personal visit, to show he was not the person 400 miles away making these purchases. Fortunately, his bank was able to cancel his card and prevent further damage. Unfortunately, this was not able to happen until after the thief had already made off with several hundred dollars of merchandise from a store.

I mentioned before that not all the monitoring in the world could prevent a theft of your credit card. I am not saying this to be negative. I bring this up because I want to re-emphasize the importance of PERSONAL responsibility when it comes to preventing theft. Many times, I hear people state they are not worried because if someone rips them off their bank will simply reimburse the funds. This is a flawed mentality. While it may be true that your bank may reimburse lost funds, it will not be *"free"*. The banks and stores will recover loses, typically in the form of increased prices or fees, which we all pay! *If you find a business that IS giving away free money, please contact me at the email address at the beginning of this book!*

∞ ∞ ∞ ∞ ∞

*"Technology gives us power, but it does not and cannot tell us how to use that power.
Thanks to technology, we can instantly communicate across the world,
but it still doesn't help us know what to say."*
~Jonathan Sacks

∞ ∞ ∞ ∞ ∞

Dealing with Your Credit Report

Did you know you are entitled to a FREE copy of your personal credit report from EACH of the Credit Reporting Agencies (CRA) each year? However, be careful: There are plenty of rip-off sites trying to trick you into purchasing their services in return for your copy of the report. Avoid the fraud artists and make sure you only use the "*official*" site for obtaining your copies:

www.ANNUALCREDITREPORT.com

∞ ∞ ∞ ∞ ∞

If you request one copy from each CRA
every three (3) months,
you will be able to get year-round coverage.
Be sure to mark your calendar!

∞ ∞ ∞ ∞ ∞

What about all those commercials you see for credit monitoring? There is no need to pay for services when you can get many of them FREE! These services offer you a valuable insight into your credit status...and even your credit scores. Two popular ones directly supported by the agencies are:

- **www.CREDITKARMA.com**
    - o   Provides monitoring of TransUnion and Equifax

- **www.CREDITSESAME.com**
    - o   Provides Monitoring of Experian

What about all the junk mail that hits your postal mailbox? Those credit offers are the result of the credit agencies selling your information to outside vendors so they can flood you with offers you never asked for. Beyond their annoyance, these unsolicited offers give credit thieves a valuable tool for taking advantage of your good credit. Luckily, it is simple, and free, to get rid of these forever. You can visit **www.OPTOUTPRESCREEN.com** and request they NOT sell your credit report information to data brokers for a period of 5 years. You would need to renew this request every five years.

Did I not say earlier that it was forever? *That is going to cost you...*the price of a stamp. Simply print, fill out, and mail the form available on the **www.OPTOUTPRESCREEN.com** web site and you will never have your information sold, unless you use another stamp and ask them to start selling you out again!

While we are talking about credit reports, please do not forget the younger ones in your life. Many statistics show that juvenile identity theft is on the rise. Children today leave the hospital with a social security number and a potential target on their diaper. Be sure you monitor your children's account to ensure they stay safe as well.

Two options I feel are great for children are (1) *"freezing"* their credit records or (2) setting up fraud alerts. Freezing your credit with credit agencies is a GREAT option for those not frequently opening new credit accounts. Fraud alerts prompts creditors to perform further verification before extending credit. You must file fraud alerts with each credit-reporting agency individually. While the freeze is a permanent solution (*until you contact the CRA to lift the freeze*), the fraud alert is only good for a short period, typically 90 days. Freeze and fraud alert procedures differ by state and can sometimes require a nominal (*$10.00 or less*) fee. Please visit the site below and search for *"Credit Freeze (your state)"* for details on how to take the steps necessary:

www.CONSUMERSUNION.org

Internet Safety Signs

Internet browsers employ several features to protect your identity while using the Internet. Making yourself aware of a few simple things can go a long way to making online shopping and banking more secure. Often people ask if, with all the online dangers I have seen, I feel safe purchasing or conducting business online. Simply put, yes I do. The reason I can say that with confidence is that I pay attention to a few things to keep myself, and my identity, safe:

- Security Warning Page

- Only Use "*My*" Shortcuts

- Internet Browser Bar

Security Warning Page. It may come as a surprise that your browser does not WANT you to visit compromised sites. It will try to give you warnings, though unfortunately people have a tendency to ignore these. One of the most obvious involves a bold alert warning that you NOT proceed due to errors. I cannot recall how many times I have heard stories from people wondering why they had problems after ignoring these warnings. If you reach a page, especially one dealing with personal/financial information, and see a page similar to the example shown...DO NOT continue! This indicates a potential issue with the web site security measures. This could include a compromise that would potentially reveal your information

 There is a problem with this website's security certificate.

The security certificate presented by this website was issued for a different website's address.

Security certificate problems may indicate an attempt to fool you or intercept any data you send to the server.

We recommend that you close this webpage and do not continue to this website.

 Click here to close this webpage.

 Continue to this website (not recommended).

 More information

Sample Website Certificate Error Warning

Only Use "My" Shortcuts. I cannot say this enough: never, ever, ever, EVER follow a link you receive in an email to ANY site dealing with YOUR personal information. This is even more important if the site in question is financial in nature. By utilizing shortcuts that I have typed personally, I can ensure that I end up where I want to be on the Internet and not where some crook wants me to go.

Internet Browser Bar. One of the first places you should look when dealing with a financial site is the address bar of your browser. It gives you some visual clues on the security status of the page visited. There are three key security "*clues*" to look for when evaluating the safety of the site. I bring this up in regards to financial sites, because these are protections normally reserved for financially related transaction sites, or those with similar privacy concerns. Sites may use one or more of the following enhanced security features:

- Colored Address Bar

- Padlock Symbol

- HTTPS Instead Of HTTP (*Without The S*)

Colored Address Bar. When securing a website for privacy protection, an increasing number of companies are opting to implement the colored address bar to give users an extra visual clue to the secured status. Sites with this feature will have a green colored address bar. It will change to green to let you know the site is safe and secured with an item called an "*SSL certificate*". This is a certificate obtained to verify the legitimacy of the website (*i.e. they are who they say they are*) and used to securely encrypt (*i.e. scramble*) your communications to ensure privacy. As an additional defense, if there is an error with the certificate the bar color will change to red.

It is important to note that not all secured sites utilize the altered color for the address bar. This additional feature costs more when purchasing the certificate, so not all companies use it. Its presence does not indicate increased security over non-colored address bars. It is simply an additional visual feature to aid users in knowing the security status of the web site visited.

Padlock Symbol. When accessing a website secured by the previously mentioned SSL certificate the browser screen will also show a padlock symbol. Depending on your version of browser, this image could be in a lower corner of the screen or very close to the address on the address bar. Its presence indicates the presence of additional security measures to protect your information.

HTTPS Instead of HTTP (Without the S). A secured website will also have the address name appear a bit different. The added "S" at the beginning of the web address means "*Secure*". This indicates the web site uses the SSL certificate we mentioned earlier to secure your communications.

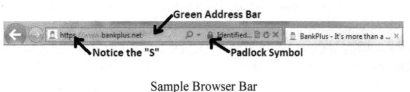

Sample Browser Bar

✝ ✝ ✝ ✝ ✝

Social Media Concerns

How much information do you reveal about yourself on social media? Could I discover your favorite color or the mascot of your high school? Would I be able to learn your mother's maiden name? If these questions sound familiar, they should. These commonly asked security questions assist web sites when verifying your identity. With this little bit of information I could potential access your entire social and financial kingdom. It seems a lot to be protecting and yet so many will simply give away the information without a second thought.

Every time I scroll through my social media feeds, I shake my head in disbelief at all the information people will share. Do not get me wrong – I like social media too. Nevertheless, those *"Learn about Your Friends"* lists make me cringe as I see many questions in them used by banks and other secure web sites to protect identities. Are we TRULY close friends with everyone in our friends list? Are we close friends with EACH of their friends, and so on?

If you are concerned with protecting your identity, and those of your family, think before you share. While it is great to get to know each other, not everyone needs to know everything. Treat your information on social media much as you would your underwear: Do not tell everyone what you have, be mysterious, and if an accident occurs, be sure to change (*your password*) immediately.

∞ ∞ ∞ ∞ ∞

*"One day soon the Gillette Company will announce
the development of a razor that,
thanks to a computer microchip,
can actually travel ahead in time and shave beard hairs
that don't even exist yet"*

~ Dave Barry

∞ ∞ ∞ ∞ ∞

Frequently Asked Questions

∞ ∞ ∞ ∞ ∞
"We had the Greatest Generation, the Boomers,
Generation X, Generation Y, and now:
Generation Text."
~ Greg Tamblyn
∞ ∞ ∞ ∞ ∞

This is a rather fun section of the book. As I researched information, I came across plenty of smaller tidbits of information that, while not big enough for a whole chapter, were definitely worthy of an *"honorary mention."* In addition, during this same time family, friends, and co-workers asked me questions and I realized they would be nice additions as well. To borrow a term from my corner of the country, I consider this section *"Lagniappe"* (*lagniappe is a New Orleans term for "a little something extra"*!) for the readers. If there are questions YOU want answered, please feel free to contact me at the e-mail address on the copyright page of the book.

BETA Software

Q. I keep reading about BETA software, especially in regards to my mobile phone and tablet. What is BETA software, and is it safe for me to use?

A. BETA software is a version of the software for the device that is almost ready for public release but may still have a couple of issues. Generally, manufacturers of the software will release it in this form so that a small section of the general public can test drive it and help locate any bugs that may not have been caught during development.

In regards to the safety of BETA software, I must answer the question with a question. Do you consider yourself an above-novice user? I would generally NOT recommend anyone run BETA software without a basic understanding and comfort with software that may be less than stable. It is common for this pre-release software to result in crashing, screen freezes, or even a loss of data.

Storing Photos in the Cloud

Q. Of all the files on my computer, it seems photos (*and videos*) seem to grow the fastest and take up the most space. I see many cloud providers advertising photo storage. Is this something I should look into?

A. The digital camera has caused a virtual tsunami of data growth since hitting shelves across the world. As each generation of camera steps forward, we see the file size of the pictures increase as well. With all this growth in data, it can be rather hard to manage it on your home computer. This is an area I see cloud computing stepping up to the plate and taking management to the next level.

As we mentioned in the previous chapter, cloud services give us the ability to grow as needed to fit our needs instead of a one-size-fits-most approach. We see this best illustrated when we discuss the storage of photos and video. Whether you have a few dozen or a few thousand, there is definitely a solution available to help. Moreover, many of the services are free, part of an existing subscription you may have, or available for a nominal fee. A few of the more popular choices:

- Google® Photos
- Amazon Cloud Drive Photos
- Flickr

Google® will give you unlimited space to store your photos IF you use their compression technology (*photos over 16MB in size will be compressed, though anything smaller remains at original size and quality*), which should be more than satisfactory for all but the professional photographers in the audience. With the power of Google's® search engine it should come as no surprise that the service will make assigning categories and searching your photos as easy as finding the menu for the restaurant that everyone at the office was discussing today. Desktop and mobile apps are included, and simple to use as we see from the many Google® products.

Amazon Cloud Drive photos is available to all Amazon Prime members, but for others the unlimited storage space will cost around $12.00 (*as of this writing*) to gain access to the service. Like Google® Photos, Amazon will automatically compress photos exceeding certain sizes (*13MB as of this writing*). Again, this would not affect a majority of users. It allows free synchronization from mobile or PC platforms, so getting your pictures uploaded becomes simply a matter of Internet speed and access.

Flickr, a part of the Yahoo family, starts you off with 1TB (*Terabyte*) of storage for free, which is enough to hold 300,000 pictures (*3MB each*). While less than unlimited, this is a decent amount of space, and more than enough for most users. Flickr is great if a majority of your photo uploads come from your mobile device, as batch uploading is included free. On the downside, there is a fee charged if you want this same batch feature to work from your home computer. As with the other sites, you can pay a small fee for enhanced features or additional storage as needed

Besides the advantages of having your photos stored in the cloud safe from disaster, these services provide a simple way to share your memories with family and friends. Security is also common among these programs, ensuring others only see what you allow them to see.

In Case of Emergency

Q. Recently I was speaking with a friend of mine and we were discussing how the phone now has become as much of a common accessory as a watch and wallet. With so much information at our fingertips, is there anything it can do for us in case of an emergency?

A. While having your phone handy is obviously a great tool to call 911, there is another less-known feature that can give medical responders vital information about you and any health conditions should you be unable to tell them personally.

Access to your vital medical history, medications, and contacts can be the difference between life and death. While some of us may wear medical ID bracelets to help with the most crucial of information, your iPhone can be vital link to the information for those who need it most.

Dispatchers are advising paramedics to look to your smart phone for vital emergency information, such as medical conditions, allergies, medications, and emergency contact information. This information, once set up, is visible from your locked phone when they swipe right and go to the "*Emergency*" icon. (*This option NOT available or visible on the screen until AFTER you enter your information*). The steps below will walk you through setup on an Apple® device (*requires iOS 8 or newer*). Steps would be similar for Android:

- Click on the HEALTH icon on your iPhone
- On the bottom-right click on MEDICAL ID
- Click on CREATE MEDICAL ID
- Fill in pertinent information useful in a medical emergency
- Make sure that the option for "*Show When Locked*" is ON

In case of an emergency First Responders can now access vital information from your iPhone.

Disposing of Properly

Q. I recently upgraded my (*insert technology device name here*). How can I dispose of it properly? I want to be environmentally friendly while also protecting myself from data loss.

A. Being responsible to our environment when disposing of electronics is definitely the right thing to do. All of the chemicals and components involved can be hazardous no matter what part of the country you live. Two places come to mind when I think of proper disposal: Recycling yards and electronics store. Both of these places would be an excellent resource for making sure your old device(s) are properly disposed of and not endangering the world where we all live and work.

We must also mention the protection of yourself from data loss. We must not forget that while we used our devices they could have held sensitive information. Use caution when getting rid of old technology like a computer or your cell phone. It is easy to recover your information even if you "*think*" you have erased (*formatted*) the device. I have heard many horror stories of people who sold their old computer only to soon discover someone stole their identity or posted personal information they thought long gone. When dealing with these, physical destruction is a great way to ensure that computer hard drive can no longer reveal your grandmas secret cookie recipe (*or last year's tax return*!)

About the Author

As Chief Technology Officer (CTO) and owner of TechKnolutions, LLC, Wiltz Cutrer has more than 20 years in the information technology (IT) field. TechKnolutions, LLC provides networking, security auditing, system repair, and technology consulting along with Continuing Professional Education (CPE) courses to professionals across the nation.

Wiltz started his IT career in the US Navy as a Cryptologic Technician (CTM). Still active professionally in the IT field, he applies his experience to more than just the datacenter. He has spoken at several conferences on the effective implementation and utilization of technology. Additionally, he founded (*and is past president of*) the Mississippi Technology Users Group (MSTUG), which unites IT personnel to promote efficiency in digital solutions.

A speaker at numerous conferences on the effective implementation and utilization of technology, he is also the co-host of the weekly "*Everyday Tech*" show on MS Public Broadcasting (**www.mpbonline.org/everydaytech**). He utilizes his enthusiasm and understanding to inspire and educate, executing diverse methods to provide a "*real-world*" view of the digital age.

Writing his first book, "*Don't Throw IT ~ Get to Know IT*", Wiltz explains technical matters for the non-technical, bringing that which he has successfully taught in the classroom to the reader. Using analogies and humor, he explains things such as computer security, Internet safety, and computer repair in a way even his mother-in-law can understand.

Married to Kristen, they have two children (*Wiltz III and Izabella)*, and proudly call Flowood, Mississippi home.

Be Sure You Check Out The 1st Book In the "Know IT" Series:

Available on Amazon

in eBook and Print

What Folks Are Saying About
"Don't Throw IT ~ Get To Know IT"

"I cannot thank the author enough for writing an easy to read book. He explains everything in simple to understand terms."

~ C.M. Cameron

"There are also loads of practical tips offered in this book. I now know how to keep my computer safe, troubleshoot problems that occur, and make it run faster."

~ A. Foster

"I appreciated the non-Technical and easy to understand tips, the suggested sites and applications, and the author's sense of humor."

~ Andrea

"The next time someone expresses frustration working with their computer, or struggling to "keep up" with the latest and greatest, I am steering them towards this book."

~ ITGal71

"There is so much helpful information included, from anti-virus/anti-malware recommendations, to choosing a router."

~ K. Cox

∞ ∞ ∞ ∞ ∞

"Th-Th-The, Th-Th-The, Th-Th...
That's all, folks!"

~Porky Pig

∞ ∞ ∞ ∞ ∞

www.ingramcontent.com/pod-product-compliance
Lightning Source LLC
Chambersburg PA
CBHW071218050326
40689CB00011B/2363